Growing Up in Stages

WITHDRAWN

EMOTIONAL
DEVELOPMENT
OF THREE- AND
FOUR-YEAR-OLDS

Susan A. Miller, EdD

Gryphon House
www.gryphonhouse.com

Published by Gryphon House, Inc.
P. O. Box 10, Lewisville, NC 27023
800.638.0928; 877.638.7576 (fax)
Visit us on the web at www.gryphonhouse.com.

Bulk Purchase
Gryphon House books are available for special premiums and sales promotions as well as for fund-raising use. Special editions or book excerpts also can be created to specifications. For details, call 800.638.0928.

Disclaimer
Gryphon House, Inc., cannot be held responsible for damage, mishap, or injury incurred during the use of or because of activities in this book. Appropriate and reasonable caution and adult supervision of children involved in activities and corresponding to the age and capability of each child involved are recommended at all times. Do not leave children unattended at any time. Observe safety and caution at all times.

Library of Congress Cataloging-in-Publication Data
The Cataloging-in-Publication Data is registered with the Library of Congress for ISBN 978-0-87659-723-1.

DEDICATION

For Owen—my amazing, playful, and creative grandson, who provided so many of the delightful scenarios in these pages.

PRAISE FOR SUSAN A. MILLER'S BOOKS IN THE GROWING UP IN STAGES SERIES

SHARON MACDONALD,
author and educator

Susan has been a personal friend and a resource for me since my classroom days teaching four-year-olds in San Antonio, Texas, and on through my years on the road speaking to teachers about the ages and stages of early childhood development. I always sought out her opinions and insights. Now I do not have to call her. I have her books!

Her understanding of social, cognitive, and emotional development in young children is unrivaled. She explains ages and stages in her unique way—clean, simple, honest. She is a gifted writer with real empathy and understanding for her subjects—children.

Susan Miller's books belong in the personal library of any early childhood teacher. Buy them.

DEBBIE VERA
PhD, associate professor and chair of the Department of Educator and Leadership Preparation, Texas A&M University

While reading the scenarios, I could easily see how all three domains in this series— emotional, social, and cognitive development—are interdependent. This series provides a holistic view of the child and really helps the reader to understand the overlap of development into each domain.

The writing style is personal and engaging for teachers.

CONTENTS

ACKNOWLEDGMENTS

My family—Peter, Gregg, Owen, and Adam—for their support and patience.

My typist of many years, Karen Epting, for her professionalism and sense of humor.

Librarian Julie Daigle, for her invaluable assistance with researching children's books.

Diane Ohanesian, for encouraging me to write this series.

Gryphon House staff members Stephanie Roselli, for answering my many questions; Terrey Hatcher, for her thorough and very thoughtful editing; and Anna Wilmoth, for her assistance with details and publicity.

INTRODUCTION

For the past thirty-some years, my very special creative thinking spot has been my tiny writing cottage in Vermont overlooking Lake Dunmore. Each summer, as soon as I walk down to the edge of the lake and look out over the tranquil water, then smell the fresh leafy and piney scents oozing from the Green Mountains, I feel the stress of the past year slowly leaving my body. Emotionally, I feel I have become completely relaxed. Feeling so pleasantly renewed, it is easy to focus and turn my thoughts to writing about young children. I am reminded how preschoolers' moods and emotions are also influenced by their senses and surroundings.

It is not very difficult to know exactly how preschoolers are feeling. They truly wear their emotions for all to see! What a huge range of emotions they display—including big smiles, scowling frowns, and exaggerated pouts.

Preschoolers' emotions quickly shift from one moment to the next. A four-year-old can be laughing loudly while telling a joke. At the same time, a three-year-old, who is not always able to control his feelings, might become angry and kick the jokester because he is upset that his friend insulted him and hurt his feelings. Their emotions are all about a particular instant in time and the specific situation. In just a few minutes everything can change, and the preschoolers are all smiles as together they race their toy trucks down the sand pile.

What You Will Notice

With their increasing language skills, three- and four-year-olds are learning to use applicable words, such as *happy*, *mad*, or *sad*, to explain how they and others are feeling about a situation.

Not terribly empathetic, a three-year-old understands how she feels when she wants a toy and her friend refuses to give it to her. Because she is still egocentric, she doesn't understand how her friend is feeling. She may even respond with physical actions, such as hitting and pushing. A four-year-old, however, is more tuned into her friend's emotions, and she is able to react more kindly as she experiments with various ways to resolve conflicts, such as sharing or compromise.

Still working on becoming independent, three-year-olds have poor impulse control and often rely on help from adults. Four-year-olds, however, ooze confidence as they enjoy showing off how powerful they are. They love to challenge themselves by taking risks and testing limits in a bid for independence and being the center of attention.

Another common challenge among preschoolers is handling conflicts over possessions. When they get upset over these types of conflicts and a perceived lack of attention, they may react with anger. Three-year-olds tend to be self-centered and react without thinking about their peers. In these situations, they might respond physically or ignore the problem. More verbal, four-year-olds are apt to resort to name-calling or berating themselves.

As preschoolers develop emotional skills, they show fear in many ways, depending on their temperaments. They might withdraw from a situation, show fake bravery, or tell the teacher why they are afraid. Some common fears are monsters, and thunder and lightning. They are learning to distinguish between fantasy and reality. As a result of being anxious and fearful, some preschoolers may exhibit shy behaviors.

It is entertaining to observe preschoolers as they develop their sense of humor. They find ridiculous things incredibly amusing and love to twist words all around to sound silly. Commonly expressing their emotions in the extreme, they might yell and have huge temper tantrums when they are angry, yet their unabashed joy over a joke or potty humor may make them and their buddies laugh hysterically for what seems like forever.

Separation and loss are emotional events that cause preschoolers to struggle with their feelings. They find it difficult to deal with situations that they seem to have little or no control over. How they manage depends on their needs, their experiences, and your assistance.

This book is designed to help you understand the emotional reactions of preschoolers in your care and learn useful strategies for encouraging developmentally appropriate behaviors among children who are three and four.

As You Read This Book

As you start each chapter, you will find a definition for the chapter's theme. As you read on, you may wish to think about and add your own definitions on sticky notes.

Next are some highlights of developmental milestones of three- and four-year-olds. These will help you understand the stage of emotional development that a preschooler is functioning in during a specific time.

Then I will share some scenarios related to the chapter topic. These snapshot views are taken from events that happened with the children in my various classrooms (names changed, of course), from observations that I have been fortunate enough to make in preschool programs around the United States and abroad, and from special memories of my grandsons at particular three- and four-year-old stages. Related to the different scenarios are explanations of the stages to help you understand why a behavior or action is or is not occurring at that specific time. As we are all aware, individual preschool children may develop at different rates—some a little slowly, and others more rapidly.

Although I would like very much to have a face-to-face conversation with each reader, that of course is not possible. So what I have tried to do, as the author and a teacher, is to write in a conversational tone discussing the stages that young children go through. Rather than burdening you with heavy research and theoretical references, I have attempted to keep the flow of observation and application light and practical.

Next you will discover guidance specifically for you, the teacher or caregiver. The section called What You Can Do is designed to serve as a springboard by providing exciting curriculum activities or helpful teaching strategies for you to try with the children in your care. Feel free to build on these ideas and write on sticky notes to make this section your own.

The Other Aspects to Consider—Alerts section deals with some of the types of circumstances you might have questions about, such as recognizing when children are not quite in step with the emotional-development milestones for their age. This may indicate that you or a child's parents should consider seeking professional assistance for answers.

The ideas in the Activities for Parents to Try at Home portion are fun, easy-to-accomplish adventures appropriate for parents to explore with their children. You may wish to share these ideas with parents during conferences, online, in your newsletter, or by posting on a bulletin board. If you like, ask parents to share their own ideas on the topic and to provide photos of the activities for everyone to enjoy afterward.

Finally, a special section suggests fascinating books to read with children. All of the literature is related to the chapter topic and just begs you and the children to look at the enticing pictures, talk about the words, and enter into a dialogue about what is happening on the pages. Research shows that reading to young children is the most important way to stimulate their desire to become readers.

As you read this book, I hope you enjoy your adventures observing young children and learning how various emotional-development milestones affect the different stages of the lives of three- and four-year-olds.

1

DEVELOPING
KINDNESS AND
EMPATHY

Kindness—showing concern for others, being helpful to someone, being considerate
Empathy—understanding and sharing others' feelings

et's look at a snapshot of what you might observe as three- and four-year-olds grow emotionally. Although not all children develop at the same rate or achieve specific milestones at the same time, here is what you can probably expect to see as preschoolers develop their ability to show kindness and empathy.

- Three-year-olds may appear unkind.
- Three-year-olds don't like to apologize.
- Three-year-olds have limited empathetic resources.
- Four-year-olds may exhibit sympathy.
- Four-year-olds like to help friends.
- Four-year-olds are learning about reciprocity.

Now, let's think about some scenarios that might be happening in your classroom as preschoolers develop their empathy and interact with one another in kind and unkind ways.

Hailey, a four-year-old, is decorating the last piece of special, folded, sparkly paper. A small group of girls are making get-well cards for Chloe, a friend in the hospital. By the time Ivana joins the others, all of the paper is gone. Upset, she pouts and exclaims, "What can I use? Chloe will think I don't like her!" Sensing Ivana's utter distress, Hailey hands her a big envelope and says, "Ivana, don't be sad. We need a really good drawer. You can draw a picture and make this envelope for the cards look beautiful!" Ivana smiles as Hailey tells her, "Don't forget, an artist always signs her work. Then Chloe will know it's from you."

Children are born with an amazing capacity for empathy. However, it is also possible for them to learn to be empathetic over time and with practice. Empathy needs to be a natural action and something spontaneous that comes from the young child, such as Hailey's kind offer of a way to include Ivana when she perceived how miserable Ivana was feeling. With well-developed verbal skills, Hailey suggested a wonderful strategy to not only make Ivana feel better but also solve her problem. By the time preschoolers are four, they are less egocentric and their executive-functioning skills foster their ability to take on another child's perspective.

If preschoolers know each other or are good friends, like the children in Hailey's group, they are more apt to respond to a troubling situation with kindness. They want to please their friends. For instance, Ivana was worried that her friend Chloe's feelings might be hurt if she thought Ivana didn't care enough to send a card to her. However, preschoolers may not be as spontaneous or caring with children they do not know as well.

In another part of the classroom, three-year-old Michael is building with table blocks. As he continues building, his sprawling space city begins to seriously encroach on Carlton's farm. When the blocks touch, Carlton pushes Michael's blocks away, and this topples a portion of Michael's city. Surprised and angry, Michael yells, "Carlton, you are bad!" Ms. Wynn arrives and assesses the situation. She states, "Carlton, look at the mess. Michael is unhappy. If you want to continue to play, you must apologize to Michael and help him rebuild his city."

For a three-year-old like Carlton, it is very difficult cognitively to understand the things the teacher is telling him. At this age, it is hard for him to perceive another child's feelings when he is not feeling the same way at the moment. Emotionally, he is not able to exhibit empathy and may even appear unkind. First of all, when the teacher gives him a moral directive, such as apologizing to another child to show he cares and is sorry for his actions, he probably doesn't understand why because he is the one who is upset by Michael's tactic.

Emotional Development of Three- and Four-Year-Olds

He is frustrated to hear that maybe he can't stay at the block table when, after all, it was his space that was being invaded. Besides, Carlton really wasn't concerned with Michael's project, as he was absorbed in his own activity.

Outside, Bethany trips on the playground and falls down, cutting her knee. Three-year-old Andrea just stands and watches wide-eyed as the blood stains Bethany's torn pants. Still very egocentric, Andrea does not exhibit any kind behaviors, such as consoling Bethany physically with a hug or helping her up. It is difficult for Andrea to overcome her own anxiety caused by the situation of the fall and seeing the blood. Using her limited empathetic resources, another three-year-old demonstrates a compassionate behavior in physical and nonverbal ways by patting Bethany gently as the child's mommy does to her. Even though Erik, a three-year-old, doesn't help Bethany, he runs to tell the teacher so she can provide assistance.

During sociodramatic play, opportunities frequently present themselves that encourage acts of kindness. As preschoolers begin to interact with each other in make-believe play, using themes involving conflicts, rescue, and sudden threats can encourage kindness and enable children to practice caring roles as they develop their prosocial skills. For example, when Jonathan yells, "Fire!" the boys put on their helmets and rush to get out the ladders. After they act out rescuing a frightened baby from a burning building, they perform CPR before handing the baby to her happy mom.

Instead of always focusing on materials and possessions, four-year-olds are beginning to enjoy helping their friends. Best friends Theo and Bryan are designing helicopters using wooden construction toys. When they realize there are only a few connectors left, they have a lively talk. Theo tells his buddy, "Okay. You can use them to finish your rotor. But don't forget, I let you have them to help you out!" Maybe Theo hopes this act of kindness will pay off later on when he needs to call in a favor. Both boys are learning about the process of reciprocity.

Although preschoolers are well aware that everyone has feelings, it is important for children to know that some reactions to feelings may not be all right. Unkind responses may hurt others' feelings. Perception is an essential part of empathy. Often, young children laugh at a situation because others are laughing, such as when a child puts his shirt on backward, or they are happy an incident didn't happen to them, such as accidentally wetting their pants. Quite curious, preschoolers might comment on something in a way that may appear inappropriate or unkind. For example, Lorraine says loudly to her teacher, "What's wrong with George? Doesn't he know you aren't supposed to put a button [his hearing aid] in your ear?" It is important for teachers to help young children discuss and understand their emotional and cognitive concerns so they can learn to be kind.

What You Can Do

- **Involve children in "Oh, no! What can we do?" stories.** Periodically, make up short stories for the children to finish. Ask them to tell how they might help the character. For instance, "Rosa is squeezing glue on her collage paper. The top comes off, and glue goes all over her colored construction-paper shapes and the table. Upset, Rosa starts crying. Oh, no! What can we do?" Encourage the children to offer kind and empathetic suggestions. They might suggest hugging Rosa, giving her a paper towel to wipe up the glue, or getting her new paper and more colored shapes.

- **Mentor caring behavior.** Help young children become aware of when others need assistance. You might ask, "Why do you think Maggie is frowning? How can you help her?" After children are aware of the situation, analyze and try solutions with them.

- **Set up cooperative group projects.** Offer activities with materials that children need to share or work on together to complete, such as puzzles with a number of pieces. A train set or a city built with Lego bricks and many other parts can encourage children to negotiate and be empathetic to the various designers' construction needs.

- **Display posters that promote a climate of kindness.** Take photos of children in the classroom involved in kind acts—giving a friend a doll to hold or tying another child's shoelaces. Blow up the pictures and prominently display them as an inspiration to be kind.

- **Develop a kindness list.** Brainstorm and list ways to make your classroom environment kinder. When a kind act is performed, check off the item and write down the names of the empathetic children and their fortunate recipients. Add happy-face stickers!

- **Participate in an altruistic project.** Encourage the children to think how they might bring happiness into others' lives. For example, provide art supplies for the children to decorate tray favors for a hospital or nursing home to cheer up patients during holiday time.

OTHER ASPECTS TO CONSIDER—ALERTS

- **Recognize that saying sorry is an ineffective strategy.** You need to focus on a young child's personal feelings first as a jumping-off place for relating to others' feelings. If a child is forced to say "I'm sorry" to another child but doesn't understand why, the request may backfire. The insincerity of this coerced request may send a message to a preschooler that his feelings don't really matter at all.

- **Be aware of don'ts.** To foster a kind environment, put a positive spin on your requests. If you find yourself saying "Don't hit" to the preschoolers, change your negative wording to let the children know what you want them to do instead. For instance, you might say, "Use your words. Tell Jared what you want. Say, 'I want the ball now!'"

- **Involve young children in the affective process.** Instead of dictating solutions that you think are best, assist preschoolers in exploring how others are feeling and what they could do to make them feel better. Ask open-ended questions such as "Why do you think Martin looks angry?" or "How might we work together to fix the broken toy?" This helps preschoolers learn to be empathetic and practice responding with kindness.

- **Be aware of serious unkind acts.** If a young child continuously performs unkind acts (physically hurting others, overzealously teasing, or destroying equipment), you should meet with his parents or a school counselor to ascertain if there might be emotional or cognitive reasons for his behavior that need special attention.

ACTIVITIES FOR PARENTS TO TRY AT HOME

- **Model kindness.** Throughout the day, talk about kind acts with your child as they naturally occur. For example, "Look at Janice's face. She's feeling sad. She has scraped her knee. Let's put a Band-Aid on her boo-boo. Now she feels better."
- **Make your home a warm, friendly place.** Provide a caring environment. For times when your child might feel lonely or sad, offer a soft quilt to wrap up in and fluffy, soft animals to hug. Supply puppets so your child can act out her angry or hurt feelings. A rocking chair is a wonderful spot to unwind in and sing happy songs together.
- **Volunteer with your child.** Be kind and help others together. Deliver lunch and brighten up a senior citizen's day with a program such as Meals on Wheels. Weed a sick neighbor's garden to show you care about her.

- **Shower your pet with kindness.** If you see that your dog is scratching because he is being annoyed by pesky fleas, help your child give him a bath or use a handheld shower spray.
- **Discuss messages on TV; watch programs together.** Identify when characters perform kind or unkind actions. Ask your child how he might act in the same situation.
- **Act out scenarios.** Use props to dramatize your child's favorite stories. For instance, encourage her to try out kind and unkind roles from a book such as *Cinderella*. Ask how these contrasting roles make her feel.

Related Books to Read with Children

Freeman, Don. 1968. *Corduroy*. New York: Viking Press.

Henkes, Kevin. 2008. *Chrysanthemum*. New York: Mulberry Books.

Hinds, Patricia Mignon. 1996. *My Best Friend*. New York: Golden Books.

Hoose, Phillip, and Hannah Hoose. 1998. *Hey, Little Ant*. Berkeley, CA: Tricycle Press.

Minarik, Else Holmelund. 1957. *Little Bear*. New York: Harper & Bros.

2

GAINING
INDEPENDENCE

Independence—freedom of control or freedom from the influence of others

As three- and four-year-olds develop independence, you are likely to see the following types of behaviors:

- Three-year-olds are enthusiastic about trying out new things, but they will rely on adults to assist them in mastering various skills.
- Three-year-olds feel comfortable asking friends for help as they strive for independence.
- Three-year-olds gain confidence and feel successful when they perform independently.
- Four-year-olds use their thinking skills to solve problems independently as they arise during play or other interactions.
- Four-year-olds still want to please adults and may feel slightly guilty if they feel they have disappointed them.
- Four-year-olds may wish to ignore the rules if they feel an adult is trying to restrict their newfound independence.

The following anecdotes will help you understand the types of interactions that might be happening in the classroom as preschoolers explore their independence.

Three-year-old Abigail picks up a *kalimba*, an African musical instrument, from the shelf in the music center. Excited, she says, "I love how this sounds. I can make this play music!" Abigail tries strumming the metal "keys." Then she gently pounds them with her fist. Baffled when she cannot create the desired sounds, she calls for the teacher to help her make the kalimba play music. Meanwhile, four-year-old Roberto intervenes and shows Abigail how to press down and release each

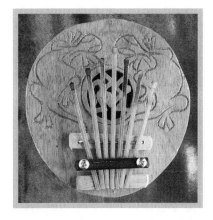

metal strip with the fingers to create delightful, melodic sounds. All smiles, Abigail says, "Thanks." Feeling good about his accomplishment, Roberto tells her and their teacher, "I fooled around with this thing yesterday."

With a clearer sense of self now that she is no longer a toddler, Abigail is enthusiastic about trying out new things by herself. Even though she has heard the kalimba and observed from the sidelines as her teacher played it, Abigail still relies on her teacher in a type of *instrumental dependency* to assist her in mastering various skills. Three-year-olds, like Abigail, feel quite comfortable asking adults and friends for guidance as they strive for independence.

In a form of *emotional dependency*, three-year-olds often enjoy sitting right next to their teachers for physical support and verbal suggestions. After a little assistance from Roberto and the teacher, Abigail becomes excited as she practices actually playing the kalimba with the appropriate finger movements. Feeling successful, she quickly gains confidence as she performs independently of others.

Confident four-year-olds, like Roberto, love to jump right in and experiment with things. They use their thinking skills to solve problems independently while they mess around. With persistence and his better-developed fine motor skills, he figured out how to master plucking the kalimba's metal strips. Proudly, he shares his newly developed skills.

Although adult approval is not mandatory for four-year-olds as they work toward independence, they still want to please their teachers and parents and may feel a little guilty if they feel they have disappointed them. For example, when a cup of sand that Emily has just poured for herself spills all over the rug as she trips while trying to carry it, she becomes frustrated. Wishing to be self-reliant, she does not want to accept any adult help in cleaning up the spill.

Preschoolers may assert their rights or flex their muscles with great pride or confidence as they act quite independently. Sometimes they make a decision to tackle a project their own way, even if this means excluding a friend or not sharing a special piece of equipment. For example, because Werner brought in his dad's old toy steam shovel to show the class after the teacher read the book *Mike Mulligan and His Steam Shovel* by Virginia Lee Burton, he feels he should be the only one to dig a foundation in the dirt pit on the playground, even though his best friend wants to join in.

Along with learning to feel powerful while asserting his independence, a preschooler may respond to others with an emphatic "No!" When Randy, a three-year-old, snatches up the bucket of Lego bricks, Liam pulls them back. He tells Randy, "No! They are mine. I had them first!" With increased communication skills, three-year-olds are beginning to try to gain control with verbal assertions, rather than physical actions such as hitting or having a tantrum.

Feeling rather self-important, four-year-olds enjoy testing the limits in their quest for independence. They often ignore the rules in an effort to do something their way. For instance, Avida's teacher tells her to slow down on her swing. Having taught herself to pump her feet in order to go high in the air, Avida defiantly responds to her teacher, "No, I don't want to!" Four-year-olds, like Avida, frequently don't want to stop something if they feel an adult is trying to restrict their newfound independence.

This conflicting type of behavior can certainly be a source of irritation between the child and her teacher or parent who cares about her safety. On the other hand, demonstrating her independence can also be positive as she makes her own decisions to make friends, explore new materials, and choose ways to solve problems.

What You Can Do

- **Make it easy.** Put materials in clear containers on low shelves to encourage independence. Provide paper towels and a dishpan with soapy water for children to clean up after themselves. Put away inappropriate or unsafe items that preschoolers should not have to make decisions about using, such as adult-sized sharp scissors.
- **Do not do things for children that they can do for themselves.** Give them time to zip up their own coats. Instead of selecting crayons for the art table, allow them to choose a medium they would like to use. Encourage them to wash their own hands before snack.
- **Encourage their independence.** Give them control over their environment and behavior when appropriate. Use positive reinforcement instead of commenting negatively about messy or failed attempts. Compliment them with a thumbs-up or a specific positive verbal message, such as "Way to go! You finished that difficult puzzle."

- **Allow plenty of time.** In order to complete certain tasks independently and not feel pressured by having to rush, preschoolers may need a few extra minutes. For instance, when learning to button her sweater, a young child might require some practice time before she accomplishes her task. While serving themselves some tricky-to-handle foods, such as peas or Jell-O, preschoolers should not feel hurried.

- **Showcase independent actions.** Take pictures of various children caring for their personal needs (hanging up a jacket or throwing away their juice cups) or taking care of the environment (watering a plant or washing paintbrushes). Create a photo album to highlight and discuss their wonderful independent behavior.

- **Offer food experiences to build self-esteem.** Encourage young children to work independently by washing vegetables, tossing salad ingredients, setting their own place at the table, and pouring glasses of milk. Supply sponges, a broom, and a dustpan for independent cleanup after eating.

OTHER ASPECTS TO CONSIDER—ALERTS

- **Encourage initiative.** It may seem easier and more practical to do things yourself because preschoolers can be very messy and clumsy with their still-developing fine motor skills and readily expanding cognitive abilities. However, it is extremely important to their emotional development to allow them to take the initiative and try to do things independently, rather than taking charge and doing a task yourself because it is neater or might save time.

- **Control your irritation over challenging behavior.** Sometimes, a preschooler's assertiveness and defiant behavior when she insists on doing something herself because she wants to feel like a big girl can be annoying. Remember, this is a very natural part of her development. It is your role to be respectful of her independence and to make sure she stays safe and doesn't hurt another child's feelings.

- **Be aware of cultural differences.** Be sensitive that in certain cultures a child's gender makes a huge difference in how a child is encouraged to develop his or her independence. Boys may be spurred on and offered ongoing chances to do things, yet girls may not be provided with the same motivation or opportunities.

Activities for Parents to Try at Home

- **Make routines predictable.** This helps your child know exactly what to expect and allows him to perform his daily tasks independently. You might draw a picture chart together to help your child remember what to do first, then next (eat breakfast, brush teeth, get dressed).

- **Keep it simple.** For toileting ease, provide clothes that are big enough for your child to pull on and off all by herself. Take pictures of hand-washing steps and create a poster to follow. A hand-pump liquid-soap dispenser encourages hand washing after toileting.

- **Use photos for a memory jog.** Sometimes your child may appear shy or uncomfortable because she does not remember people or their names. If you have photos of expected visitors, such as Li from library story time, look at them in advance. Identify the visitors and talk about the fun things your child did with them the last time they were together. This may make visitors seem more familiar and the experience less frightening for your shy child.

- **Offer interesting food choices.** Fabulous finger foods such as fresh strawberries dipped in low-fat cream-cheese spread are easy to manipulate and fun to eat. Let your child select his own fruit pieces to create an individual healthy fruit salad. Encourage him to explore unique ways to prepare his food (spread cheese on bread and roll it up for a cylinder sandwich, or use cookie cutters for fascinating sandwich shapes).

- **Offer your child jobs she can perform successfully.** Have her fill the dog's water bowl. Let her wash vegetables for a salad. Use a quilt so she can easily make up her own bed. She'll appreciate that you see her as being responsible.

- **Give your child a role in decision making.** Respect his feelings if he wishes to say no to your suggestions. Talk about a situation instead of challenging him. Together, decide between alternative solutions that are acceptable.

Related Books to Read with Children

Ashley, Bernard. 1995. *Cleversticks*. New York: Crown.

Cannon, Janell. 1993. *Stellaluna*. San Diego: Harcourt.

Carle, Eric. 1998. *Little Cloud*. New York: Philomel Books.

Henkes, Kevin. 2006. *Lilly's Purple Plastic Purse*. New York: Greenwillow Books.

Piper, Watty. 1930/2012. *The Little Engine That Could*. New York: Penguin.

3

DEALING WITH
SHYNESS

Shyness—a tendency to feel awkward, timid, or worried; an inclination to back off from connecting with others

hen three- and four-year-olds exhibit shyness, consider the following tendencies as you seek ways to help:

- Three-year-olds may naturally display shyness in large-group settings or unfamiliar places.
- Three-year-olds may learn to back away from a certain situation if they had an unhappy prior experience.
- Three-year-olds may be less assertive than older preschoolers.
- Four-year-olds may fear criticism from others and be concerned about losing control.
- Four-year-olds need unpressured time and lots of opportunities to observe from a safe place to feel comfortable.
- Four-year-olds who exhibit shyness may have a slow-to-warm-up temperament.

Now let's look more closely and view some examples of how shyness can play out in the classroom as preschoolers develop emotionally.

Well into the second month of preschool, David, a young four-year-old, still needs to sit right next to his mom first thing every morning. She helps him put together puzzle pieces at the table in the quiet area. David continues to suck the thumb on his left hand and

hunches his shoulders self-protectively. He doesn't make eye contact with the other kids playing nearby. When David's mom finally feels comfortable leaving him at school, he moves behind the book rack and peeks out hesitantly, observing story time from a safe distance.

In conversations with David's teacher, his mom explains that she, too, is shy in new situations or when she first meets people. This is not surprising because shyness can be an inherited behavior for many young children and is really an inborn temperament. Studies show that often if a child exhibits shy behavior, at least one parent is also prone to shyness.

Like David, many shy children are predisposed to a slow-to-warm-up temperament. Before they enter a new situation, they usually take a period of waiting and watching to see what is happening. They are less assertive by nature.

As a result of being anxious and fearful of new experiences, some preschoolers may exhibit a variety of shy behaviors. In general, three-year-olds react to visual fears. For example, Sophia hides behind her mom during different holidays, such as Easter and Halloween, if she sees people wearing masks or costumes. She clings tightly to her dad's legs when she's stressed, as when she's thinking about the possibility of a robber waiting for her in the dark! Three-year-olds might be very shy around a babysitter or teacher because they are afraid to have their parents leave them, especially at night.

Other fears and anxieties may exacerbate a shy child's behavior. If a child like David is afraid to take a risk or fears rejection from his classmates because he is not really sure where he should sit at story time, he may simply prefer to watch from the sidelines. Anticipating criticism from others and concerned about losing control, some shy children may decide not to participate in events at all. They may be afraid of not doing things perfectly and get stressed about expected performance, such as staying in the lines while coloring or catching a ball during a game.

Putting pressure on themselves because they feel their teacher or parents might be upset by their messiness, some shy preschoolers will not even attempt an activity such as coloring. Unfamiliar things, such as a teacher's new hair color, an unexpected substitute, or a favorite trike with a replacement wheel, can set up a red flag and can panic a shy preschooler. Inexperience with a situation or not being given helpful information (the class has to go outdoors early to play because rain is expected) can create insecure feelings for the already reluctant child.

Unfortunately, unhappy past experiences may teach a shy child to back away from certain situations. For instance, Mazie no longer feels secure just watching her peers build with blocks. Previously, two four-year-old boys teased her by chanting, "Crazy Mazie hiding under the table." A shy child, like Mazie, may feel so threatened that she doesn't speak to others and is disinclined to ask a teacher or other children for help. Displaying behavior that is introverted, Mazie may feel more comfortable playing by herself.

However, given plenty of unpressured time and lots of opportunities to observe from a perceived safe distance, many shy children can eventually enter social situations and become active participants with the help of caring adults and kind friends. Remember, it is quite common and very natural for many young children to display shyness in large-group settings or during unfamiliar situations.

On a wonderful positive note, one day a tall college freshman stood in my office doorway and introduced himself as David, a former student. I quickly realized that this was the once shy preschooler who used to peek out from behind the book rack. After chatting a bit, David laughed and said, "I'll bet you never thought you'd see me here at college—especially without my mom!"

What You Can Do

■ **Don't refer to a child's shyness.** Instead, you might explain to others, "Jane isn't quite ready to play 'Old MacDonald Had a Farm.' We'll ask her again next time." Help others be accepting of her need to wait until she's comfortable.

■ **Demonstrate ways to be sociable.** Show how to greet someone by saying "hello" or offering a smile. Engage in simple conversations. Model ways for her to enter play activities by bringing a needed truck to the block corner or adding a funnel to play in the sandbox.

■ **Provide nonthreatening one-on-one activities.** Offer a ball for him to play catch with a peer or a pop-up book for them to share together. Pair him with a puzzle buddy to interact with quietly in a relaxed atmosphere. Steer the child toward small-group projects such as making pudding for snack or building with Lego bricks.

■ **Make the child feel included.** However, make sure she isn't overwhelmed. Even if the shy child doesn't volunteer to help with a classroom job, ask her if she'd like to assist. When you sing a song with names, be sure to include the child's name so she feels a part of the class but does not feel as if she's on center stage.

■ **Create a serenity spot.** Make a special place in the classroom for children, including the shy child, to retreat to if they need some quiet, undisturbed time to calm down. Add soft pillows and huggable stuffed animals to a private, cozy little alcove created by a low divider.

Other Aspects to Consider—Alerts

■ **Be aware of labeling.** Always explaining to others that the child is shy might cause the child to feel guilty about or ashamed of her behavior. Stop and think before speaking for the child.

■ **Observe relationships carefully.** Does the child have difficulty relating to people outside of his family circle? Does he have any friends at school? You may wish to speak with his parents or a therapist for nonthreatening ways to help him feel comfortable around others.

■ **Provide support if a child seems unduly clingy.** Does the child physically hold on so that the parent cannot leave the child in group situations? Does the child follow the teacher everywhere? This young child may be extremely shy or have had difficult separation experiences and might benefit from a consultation with a therapist.

■ **Determine the level of avoidance.** Some shy children need a little time to warm up before participating in events, whereas others may stay painfully withdrawn to the point that it hampers their development. If the shy child doesn't ever speak to others, she might have selective mutism or a hearing disorder. If this is the case, suggest that the parents seek professional assistance.

Activities for Parents to Try at Home

- **Role-play future events.** So your child will know what to expect and not be taken by surprise, talk about and practice what will happen on the first day of school or at Thanksgiving dinner at Grandma's house. Use real props such as dishes and silverware.

- **Invite other children for a play date.** Your shy child may feel more comfortable playing on his home turf. It is easier for him to play with a peer later at school if he knows this friend first from a home play date.

- **Accept your child as he is.** Respect his pacing. Try not to pressure him to be more social or outgoing. Readjust your expectations if you feel you need to change his shy behavior because you were uncomfortable with your shyness when you were young.

- **Help her become more confident.** Show your support by sitting quietly near her in new situations. Never sneak out; let her know ahead of time when you must be leaving. Try pairing her with a younger child whose actions might be a little less threatening.

- **Play peekaboo.** Encourage your child to cover her face with both hands. Then, open them to peek when she is ready. Act surprised, be silly, and laugh. Have fun! Encourage her to change up her timing. You are helping her learn to be impulsive while still controlling the situation.

Related Books to Read with Children

Bracken, Beth. 2012. *Too Shy for Show-and-Tell.* Mankato, MN: Picture Window Books.

Cheng, Wen-Wen. 2013. *Maya's Voice.* CreateSpace Independent Publishing.

Morgan, Michaela. 2006. *Dear Bunny.* Frome, UK: Chicken House.

Tafuri, Nancy. 2000. *Will You Be My Friend?* New York: Scholastic.

Udry, Janice May. 1991. *What Mary Jo Shared.* New York: Scholastic.

BUILDING
CONFIDENCE

Confidence—a feeling of belief in one's own abilities

hildren naturally want to feel competent and secure, and you naturally want to help them feel that way. Although individual children develop at different rates, here is what you can expect to see with many preschoolers as they build their confidence.

- Three-year-olds believe that when they are frustrated, upset, or hurt, if they go to adults, adults will know how to make it all better.
- Three-year-olds, if stressed, will self-soothe by sucking their thumbs or fingering their favorite blankets to regain confidence.
- Three-year-olds use familiar tastes and scents, which are important sensory stimuli, to help them feel more secure.
- Four-year-olds, with their more developed skills, feel quite confident about helping others and can be rather loud and bold about it.
- Four-year-olds are more apt to be accepted during group play when they make contributions instead of insisting on having their own way.
- Four-year-olds feel confident enough to tell others if they like or do not like something.

Now let's examine some of the types of interactions that occur among preschoolers with different levels of confidence and what influences their behaviors.

Four-year-old Jason hums as he turns on the water in the sink for Patrick, a three-year-old. Patrick gleefully rubs his messy hands together under the faucet and watches in fascination as the watery green paint disappears down the drain. With a huge smile, Jason calls out loudly, "Gross! You're bleeding green slime!" Patrick responds, "Cool!" Then he proudly holds up both hands and announces to his teacher, "All clean!"

Most three-year-olds are fairly relaxed unless they are hungry, tired, or feel threatened. They are easily self-satisfied and delighted with small accomplishments, such as when Patrick was able to wash all of the green paint off his hands. Preschoolers take great pride in pleasing their teachers and parents and love to show them what they have achieved. With their more developed motor skills, four-year-olds, like Jason, feel rather confident about helping others and can be quite loud and bold about it.

If preschoolers feel frustrated, upset, or hurt, they often look to an adult to help calm them down or make them feel secure. They believe adults know just how to fix things. For instance, when Angie bumped into the corner of a table, this surprised her and bruised her arm. Mrs. Kimble held her securely and gently rubbed her arm. Soon, Angie smiled and declared, "All better!" With confidence, she smacked the offending corner and emphatically stated, "Bad table!"

If an adult isn't handy, preschoolers are frequently able to devise alternate methods to regain their confidence when they are stressed. They may try strategies such as hugging a favorite stuffed animal or fingering a special blanket. Three-year-olds, and some four-year-olds, may resort to self-soothing in a very natural way by sucking their thumbs during difficult transition times, such as naptime or heading off to school. They feel confident knowing their thumb is always there to provide stress relief.

The taste of favorite foods, such as chocolate ice cream, and familiar scents, such as the teacher's apple-blossom hand lotion, are important sensory stimuli for three-year-olds that can make them feel secure in uncomfortable situations. Rituals—such as blowing

Daddy four kisses goodbye, then going to play with Lego building materials at school—can help preschoolers anticipate what to expect next. The repeated and familiar experiences help build up their confidence.

It is not uncommon for preschoolers to have an imaginary or invisible friend. It is comforting for a young child to converse with a special imaginary friend who is a good listener while they do things together. For Ellie to feel secure in a small group during snack time, it is important to her that an extra place be set at the table so she can sit right next to her invisible friend, Bunny.

If they feel overwhelmed, four-year-olds often use fantasy play to feel in control and be powerful as they act out different scenarios. By using pretend play and their executive-functioning skills, a connection is made to outcomes, such as being able to take on challenges. When Mason sees evil rocket scientists headed his way, he quickly turns into his favorite superhero and saves the day by covering his two friends with his strong webs while they ride their scooter space ships away from the enemy.

Because it can be difficult for three-year-olds to see things from another child's point of view, they may not always approach play activities with confidence. However, unlike three-year-olds, four-year-olds do not insist on doing things their way, but instead make contributions to group play, such as bringing a flashlight to play robber. In this way, they are much more likely to have the satisfaction of being accepted. With more developed communication skills, four-year-olds can verbalize what they want. They might say, "Now it's my turn to be the ambulance driver. You can be the patient." Also, they feel confident enough to let another child know if they like or do not like something.

What You Can Do

- **Provide leadership opportunities.** Give a young child a chance to develop and show her leadership skills. This is especially important to help the hesitant or shy child build her confidence. For instance, ask her to invite several children to help her rake up the leaves, put them in the wagon, then deliver them to the mulch pile. Even doing something as simple as putting a child in charge of being the line leader when the class goes to the lobby for dismissal can make her feel special. Be sure to rotate these opportunities.
- **Provide open-ended materials.** Encourage experimentation with items such as sand, water, clay, blocks, and wood. Because there is no right or wrong way to use these materials, children can explore with confidence.

- **Offer props to act out scenarios.** By using hats, toy figurines, and puppets, a child can feel empowered and confident as he gains control of a situation. Encourage preschoolers to clearly express what they want, such as explaining, "Do not smash the control tower. Then the planes will crash!"

- **Design cozy, secure play structures.** Create a cave, house, or police station by throwing a blanket or big beach towel over a card table or clothesline. Suggest that a child slip inside this unique retreat to calm down and center her thoughts. She may wish to pretend to be a powerful character, such as a police officer or doctor.

- **Develop interesting, secure personal spaces.** Have children create make-believe bubble spaces around their bodies to dance inside so no one can bump into them. Make rectangular lines with masking tape on the table, or use plastic trays or sheets of aluminum foil to create visual boundaries for individual fingerpaintings or playdough sculptures.

OTHER ASPECTS TO CONSIDER—ALERTS

- **Be aware of stressors.** Anticipate frustrating times (feeling sleepy and needing a nap), places (waiting for a turn in the bathroom), and situations (meeting new people). Provide support; sit next to a stressed child and soothe him by rocking him and massaging his back to make him feel secure. Practice relaxation techniques; take big breaths and let them out slowly.

- **Monitor thumb sucking.** When preschoolers start to attend school, parents and teachers frequently worry that a child's thumb sucking might ruin her teeth alignment and create various difficulties with the development of her speech. However, the American Dental Association (ADA) relates that most children outgrow the practice of thumb sucking between the ages of two and four. Nevertheless, the ADA suggests that parents speak to the family dentist if a child is still thumb sucking at the time the permanent teeth arrive between four and five years old.

- **Support the imaginary friend.** Instead of ignoring this special friend, share conversations and be a good listener, if the child is comfortable with this. You'll learn a lot! Don't worry; the invisible friend will stay as long as the child has a satisfying relationship and will probably disappear by the time the child turns five.

Activities for Parents to Try at Home

- **Provide soothers.** If you can provide adhesive bandages and kisses for hurt boo-boos, this might make life a little bit better! However, if you cannot be with your child, you can provide other security soothers, such as a night-light, a juice pop to suck on, a soft quilt to hold, or quiet music to listen to. These can help build his confidence if he is stressed.

- **Pair with others.** Have your child work with a peer or older sibling who can offer tips to build confidence. For instance, my oldest grandson, Owen, shared ideas with his younger brother about what to expect in kindergarten in the fall. An older peer can model ways to enter into play and to make friends.

- **Put together puzzles.** Together, work on a puzzle to help your child create a sense of order out of the disorganized pieces. With great confidence, my youngest grandson, Adam, loves to shout out, "All done!" as he puts in the last piece and finishes a puzzle. We fondly call him "the puzzle master."

- **Scare the monsters.** To build her confidence or to scare away the monsters under the bed, teach your child to hum or sing a short tune if she is afraid of the dark. So she'll feel more secure and confident, give her a small flashlight to check the corners to make sure there are no creepy nighttime creatures.

- **Record your child's own best efforts.** It is exciting for your child to see how his behavior or skills have grown in various areas over time. For example, if your child tells you he cannot clean up all of the toys without your help, begin a graph showing how much of the room he can pick up each day by himself using his strong muscles. Over the weeks, encourage him to watch the bar graph rise, building his confidence. Award a homemade trophy or blue ribbon when he is able to pick up all of the toys independently.

- **Assign special jobs.** During family celebrations and holidays, give your child special fun projects to be in charge of that will build her confidence, such as decorating cupcakes or designing placemats with colored markers. Be sure to compliment her efforts so others will know she is responsible for creating these delightful items.

Related Books to Read with Children

Alexander, Martha. 1969. *Blackboard Bear*. New York: Dial.

Allen, Debbie. 2003. *Dancing in the Wings*. New York: Puffin Books.

Hoff, Syd. 1970. *The Horse in Harry's Room*. New York: Harper & Row.

Hutchins, Pat. 1968. *Rosie's Walk*. New York: Macmillan.

Keats, Ezra Jack. 1974. *Dreams*. New York: Macmillan.

5

TESTING LIMITS **AND** TAKING RISKS

Testing limits—pushing the boundaries to see just how far it is possible to go
Taking risks—taking a chance or doing something that could be potentially dangerous

Three- and four-year-olds often challenge the boundaries of acceptable behavior and test the patience of those they interact with. As they push their limits and take risks, you will often see some of the following behaviors.

- Three-year-olds, with their poor impulse control, may find it hard to wait or take turns.
- Three-year-olds may take risks then discover intriguing new ideas.
- Three-year-olds are seen by their peers and teachers as pushing the limits in negative ways when they grab toys or hit others.
- Four-year-olds exude confidence and enjoy showing off how powerful they are.
- Four-year-olds love to brag about their physical skills.
- Feeling empowered, four-year-olds may test limits by threatening others and calling them names to show how important they are.

Now let's take a closer look at some of the ways that preschoolers explore their world, challenge authority, and push the boundaries inside and outside the classroom.

Simply exhilarated, four-year-old Benji charges up to the top of a grassy hill on the playground. Feeling invincible, he waves his imaginary sword wildly in the air as he challenges those below him. "I'm the king of the mountain. Just try to knock me off." His teacher calls out, "Be careful, Benji. Don't do anything dangerous."

Four-year-olds ooze confidence and enjoy showing off how powerful they are. With emotions running high, they love to push everyone's buttons as they test limits

and live on the edge. Although he knows he is being defiant, Benji continues to assert himself by waving his sword. He ignores his teacher's admonishment. It is difficult for him to give up his newfound superpowers. Even though this is an actual bid for independence, teachers and parents may feel a bit uncomfortable or annoyed with this testing type of behavior because they are concerned about the safety of all of the players involved.

Feeling a bit threatened, some three-year-olds at the bottom of the hill act as observers. They carefully watch from a safe vantage point to see what others decide to do before attempting to risk making a move.

Enthusiastic, energetic preschoolers learn to develop new skills by trying out challenging activities. Sometimes preschoolers' efforts do not turn out as expected, and they may feel guilty or naughty about taking risks. For instance, with encouragement from her teacher, Jamari, a timid three-year-old, hesitantly begins to pour juice from a big pitcher for the children at the snack table. When it overflows her friend's cup and gets her shirt wet, Jamari is embarrassed. Feeling guilty about the spill, she is afraid her friend might not want to play with her. Frustrated, she is hesitant to attempt pouring again.

With their more mature physical coordination, four-year-olds love to brag about their motor skills and be the center of attention. Pushing the limits as he pumps his swing higher and higher, daredevil Josh yells, "Look at me! I'm flying so high, I'll reach the sky!" Amazingly, preschoolers appear to have an innate sense of what they can or cannot do physically and

Emotional Development of Three- and Four-Year-Olds

emotionally as they take risks. They seem to balance their sense of adventure and their desire for safety as they attempt something risky. For example, if they aren't quite ready, they may pull back from jumping off the jungle gym or sliding down the fire pole.

Still slightly egocentric, three-year-olds, with their poor impulse control, may find it difficult to wait or take a turn. Because their appropriate social and verbal skills are not yet fully developed, out of frustration they frequently hit others or grab at toys. Their peers and teachers perceive these unreasonable behaviors as pushing the limits in negative ways. On the other hand, with their increased vocabularies, know-it-all four-year-olds like to act bossy and order their playmates around because of their desire to be in control. Feeling empowered, they test limits by threatening others and calling them names to signal how important they are. When the substitute teacher, Mrs. Kulp, asked Paul to put his rest mat away, he refused and responded, "Do you know who I am? My mom is the real teacher!"

As preschoolers push the limits and learn to become risk takers, it also can be a positive experience. Intellectually, young children are able to generate intriguing new ideas. For example, in the sandbox, Michelle mixes sand and water together to make a messy cake. She then digs stones out of the flower bed and adds them to the mixture to create what she calls "rocky-road cake." Keeping safety in mind at all times, allowing young children to push the limits can encourage independent and creative thinking. When four-year-olds take risks, they often develop their problem-solving skills as they negotiate with others. This helps them learn to see things from another's point of view.

Testing limits can also teach preschoolers about learning from their own mistakes. The teacher showed Chris a fun way to tie his shoe. However, he chose to tie it in what he called a "trickier" way that he knew. After Chris took a few steps, his shoe became untied and came off, and he fell down. Through experiences such as this, preschoolers learn about the consequences of their choices.

What You Can Do

- **Begin with small risks.** Help to build children's confidence by encouraging them to try something simple at first. If a child is hesitant about getting her fingers messy, let her move fingerpaint around on paper with a cotton swab. When she feels more comfortable, she can try using one finger to paint before she uses her whole hand.
- **Pair with a buddy.** If a child appears too timid to take a risk, consider pairing him with a more confident peer. For instance, during a walk in the shadowy forest, ask Julian to hold Bryce's hand, so he can explore the nature trail with the class.

- **Show support.** When preschoolers try new ideas, acknowledge their efforts with a smile or a thumbs-up. Reinforce a child's risky effort by verbalizing the action. For example, you might say. "Look how far you jumped—all the way over the puddle!"

- **Observe abilities.** Be aware of a child's skill level. Provide choices and challenges that will be rewarding but not overly taxing. Make sure your personal feelings do not limit the children's risk taking.

- **Allow sufficient time.** Provide a flexible daily schedule to give children time to practice and experiment as they test their limits. Offer unstructured play activities as well. Making mistakes and considering how to correct them strengthens preschoolers' problem-solving abilities and builds their self-confidence.

- **Offer safe alternatives.** When a situation seems too risky, help children find safer but equally challenging opportunities. You might see that a child is building too high with wooden blocks, and you worry that they might fall and hurt someone. You could offer substitute choices such as constructing with lighter cardboard or sponge blocks. Continue the excitement while removing the danger and adding protective measures.

OTHER ASPECTS TO CONSIDER—ALERTS

- **Be careful of labeling.** When a young child's learning style is *field independent*, he likes to jump right in and mess around with the materials and activities. Because of his nature, he is sometimes labeled as impulsive, which is often perceived as a negative trait.

- **Avoid jumping to conclusions.** If a preschooler is considered to be field independent, she usually does not listen to directions first. So if things go wrong, her pushing of the limits might be blamed without evidence. Try to be respectful of this learning style as long as the child's behavior is not hurtful.

- **Recognize that overprotection can limit inquisitiveness.** Although safety is an important issue, be flexible when appropriate so as not to discourage children's risk-taking actions. Overprotecting and hovering over preschoolers may encourage them to develop fears or to constantly expect adults to solve their problems.

ACTIVITIES FOR PARENTS TO TRY AT HOME

- **Brainstorm and work together.** To expand his creative thinking, offer your child open-ended materials—such as clay, blocks, or sand—that can be used in many different ways. Share decision making about new ways to solve problems using these materials. For example, be involved by helping to steady pieces of wood as he hammers in nails to decorate a sleek space shuttle.

- **Take a risk while cooking.** Enjoy having fun taking risks by adding certain foods that don't seem to go together. For example, when you and your child are creating a cheese omelet, try adding some spinach or chopping up mushrooms and tiny pieces of tomato. Live dangerously and test the limits of your taste buds by sprinkling a touch of hot pepper sauce. Yum!

- **Ask questions.** Arouse curiosity by asking, "What if . . . ?" Offer opportunities for choices: "Which might work better, the round stone or the flat one?" Instead of dominating the conversation, be attentive to your child's responses to engage her in further inquiry.

- **Promote freedom with responsible limitations.** Provide some structure with built-in safety measures and enough flexibility to allow your child to freely explore. For example, place a resilient surface under the jungle gym to cushion any falls as he climbs and jumps.

- **Role-play scenarios.** Encourage your child to act out different risk-taking situations so she can understand them from various viewpoints. Let her be Little Red Riding Hood. Then have her pretend to be the grandma. Add props (such as a basket of goodies) to make the scene more realistic and thought provoking.

- **Discuss characters who push the limits.** Read about how characters in books behave when they test the limits. Discuss how Max breaks the rules in the popular book *Where the Wild Things Are* by Maurice Sendak. Does Max feel emancipated? What might your child do?

RELATED BOOKS TO READ WITH CHILDREN

Johnson, Crockett. 1995. *Harold and the Purple Crayon.* New York: HarperCollins.

Shannon, David. 1998. *No, David!* New York: Blue Sky.

Watt, Mélanie. 2008. *Scaredy Squirrel.* Toronto: Kids Can Press.

Wood, Don, and Audrey Wood. 1984. *The Little Mouse, the Red Ripe Strawberry, and the Big Hungry Bear.* Auburn, ME: Child's Play.

Zion, Gene. 1976. *Harry by the Sea.* New York: Harper & Row.

6

DEALING WITH **ANGER AND FRUSTRATION**

Anger—a reaction to a perceived threat that could be expressed as mild irritation, annoyance, or even strong displeasure

Frustration—the feeling of being dissatisfied or upset because of an inability to achieve something

Bursts of frustration and anger are not unusual with three- and four-year-olds. When children express these feelings, you might see some of the following types of behaviors:

- Three-year-olds often react with angry feelings when they become tense, sad, or unhappy because they are not able to do something they wish to do.
- Three-year-olds respond angrily by shoving and wiggling if they feel boxed in and jostled in small spaces.
- Three-year-olds can become frustrated if they do not understand why an adult is critical of their actions.

- Four-year-olds may react with anger when another child takes something they are playing with. They may then attempt to negotiate ways to work together to get their possessions returned.
- Four-year-olds may show their frustration with angry-looking facial expressions.
- Four-year-olds sometimes express their angry frustration by berating themselves.

Now let's get a broader perspective and examine some of the interactions you might see in the classroom that spark anger and frustration among preschoolers and how they might handle these feelings.

Outdoors, Andrew and Jian, four-year-olds, create a long fire truck with red plastic milk crates. The boys go to the storage shed to search for fire helmets. When they return, they find Ryan stacking their crates. Very angry, Andrew frowns and yells, "Dummy head! You are wrecking our perfect firefighting machine." Then, Ryan sits in a crate and refuses to move. Quite frustrated, Andrew and Jian call Ryan more names and start to topple the crates. Because they really want their special construction materials back, the boys eventually resort to negotiating with Ryan by offering to let him spray the fire hoses if he returns the crates.

When preschoolers become frustrated and embroiled in a conflict over possessions, they often react quite naturally with anger, a very basic emotion. Like Andrew and Jian, they may express their frustration with angry-looking facial expressions. Or they might verbally defend their possessions by telling the offender exactly how they feel. This frequently

includes name calling and trading insults in order to reclaim their possessions. Calling on their increased verbal skills as they work through angry feelings, older four-year-olds may even attempt to negotiate ways to work together in order to get their possessions returned. More socially skilled four-year-olds might also try compromising or taking turns with the desired items.

Armed with a big bag of tricks, frustrated and territorial preschoolers will try numerous ways to protect their space from an interloper. Andrew and Jian were angry that Ryan moved right in and destroyed their fire engine. They responded physically by pushing down Ryan's construction and would probably have considered pushing him, as well, if they had not decided to negotiate a solution. Although preschoolers may not mean to actually hurt another child, this sometimes happens when they are concentrating on regaining a prized possession or territory.

When young children become tense or feel unhappy because they are not able to do something they wish to do, they often react with angry feelings. Three-year-old Sally wanted to cut a doll's skirt with scissors to make it shorter and more beautiful. After her teacher told her not to, Sally directed her anger at the doll by throwing it on the floor and screaming, "You are a stupid old thing." Then when the teacher asked Sally to pick up the doll, the child's angry tirade continued toward her teacher. Frustrated and not feeling very compliant, Sally yelled, "You can't make me!" Used to pleasing adults, Sally felt confused because she did not understand why her teacher was critical of her actions.

Another way that preschoolers express their angry frustration is by berating themselves. Dennis mumbled about his painting by stating, "I hate the way I mixed the colors. It looks ugly like me!" Because he strives for perfection, he might even stop trying to paint altogether if he is discouraged enough. Avoidance of a task or person is a way that four-year-olds like Dennis use to escape from their frustrations.

Very active physically, four-year-olds need big spaces for their play. If they are limited by restrictive boundaries, this irritates them. On the other hand, three-year-olds may feel lost and become upset and frustrated by large spaces. However, three-year-olds and four-year-olds will respond angrily by wiggling and shoving if they feel boxed in and jostled while sitting in a small space, such as during group time.

Not at all happy if they are required to sit around and wait, preschoolers become bored and irritated very quickly. With their short attention spans, four-year-olds Marcy and Mena entertain themselves while waiting for snack by teasing Angela. At first they ignore her. Then, they exclude Angela by not allowing her to sit next to them. In singsong voices, they say, "Go away, Angie. We don't like you. Your hair smells like fish sticks." Feeling rejected, Angela cries. Then the girls hurl an additional verbal insult and tell her, "Crybaby, you can't come to our popcorn party." With hurt feelings and really angry about being excluded,

Angela responds physically by scratching the girls. All three become very frustrated and the anger escalates.

Kimberly, a three-year-old, sits near her beloved teacher, Ms. Fisher, while they put a puzzle together. When another child, Lilah, sits at the table, Ms. Fisher helps her locate puzzle pieces, too. Kimberly begins to frown and then whine because *her* teacher is complimenting Lilah and giving her what Kimberly views as extra attention. Wanting Ms. Fisher's attention for herself, Kimberly becomes exceedingly jealous and pushes Lilah's puzzle pieces on the floor. Because three-year-olds are still self-centered and not too verbal, Kimberly expresses her frustrations and annoyance by emotionally and physically acting out. In preschoolers, anger is often fueled by frustration. It occurs most frequently when they do not get the attention they wish, if their needs are not met, or if they are not able to do something.

What You Can Do

- **Demonstrate positive actions.** During problem situations model how to resolve a conflict calmly. Use a quiet voice instead of shouting, "No!" Guide the children through the steps for using negotiation strategies if they become frustrated and angry while trying to share a toy.
- **Talk things over.** If a child hurts someone's feelings, she might say, "It's okay, I was just teasing." Discuss why teasing is not fun or silly. Let preschoolers know that instead of physically responding to each other when angry by hitting, kicking, or pinching, they should verbally discuss the problem. For example, the child could ask, "Why did you take my ball?"
- **Provide plenty of time.** Rushing through activities is not satisfying and can be overly frustrating. Have prearranged signals (blinking lights or a warning song) so children will know to begin finishing up their activities.
- **Offer sufficient materials.** Sharing is difficult for preschoolers. When children fight over the same item, they become frustrated and angry. Providing duplicates of favorite pieces of equipment can help eliminate a tug-of-war or hoarding objects. However, when supplying duplicate items, it is important to make sure both are the same color, shape, and size. Otherwise, this may create a new kind of squabble when everyone wants the big ball.
- **Try out various scenarios.** If you notice that certain situations often frustrate the children (wanting to be first in line or having to take turns riding on the favorite yellow tricycle), try role-playing various solutions. Help them see that they might find several answers to a problem. Practice ways to calm down (taking deep breaths or counting to three) when they become angry.

OTHER ASPECTS TO CONSIDER—ALERTS

- **Watch out for signs of bullying.** If a child is in a constant state of anger or always feeling frustrated and seems to act out with violent behaviors, you may wish to observe and record his actions. It is important to share these during parent–teacher conferences or in ongoing discussions. There may be certain cues, such as saying "freeze" and tapping his shoulder, that you can use to help him stop a certain behavior or leave a situation before his frustration or anger escalates.

- **Work with a counselor.** If a preschooler appears to constantly tease or target (verbally or physically) a specific child, such as one who is weaker or younger, she may need help with her behavior-management skills from a professional. If you suspect that a child is being bullied, he may also need to learn coping strategies, such as using his voice to say, "Stop!" or "That is mine!" Another simple coping technique for him to try is to turn around and walk away, thereby ignoring the bully.

- **Be aware of personality traits and developmental stages.** If one child seems to react negatively to another child or to a situation, that does not mean that he is a bully. For instance, depending on their age or social maturity, three-year-olds are more apt to respond physically by grabbing a possession or shoving a person, and four-year-olds often react verbally by yelling insults and name calling. How aggressively or quickly a child responds may depend on temperament. Differences in culture and gender also can affect children's interactions.

ACTIVITIES FOR PARENTS TO TRY AT HOME

- **Supply sock-it-to-me pillows.** Stuff pillowcases with crumpled newspapers or use old pillows as punching bags to relieve frustration when your child feels like hitting something. Try alternative ways to relieve stress, such as pounding clay or stomping in a leaf pile. Jumping on sheets of bubble wrap is a sure way to turn anger into laughter with each series of pops! Kneading bread dough together and then smelling the warm, yeasty fragrance of the homemade bread baking is a fabulous way to ease stress.

Emotional Development of Three- and Four-Year-Olds

- **Make expectations clear.** Your child will be less frustrated if she knows why you don't want her to use the glitter. Tell her that it might get in her eyes, rather than declaring, "No glitter!" Eliminate unwanted surprises by letting your child know right up front what you want. Say, "Please keep the sand inside the box."

- **Provide peace chairs.** If two children become very angry, offer each one a seat in a peace chair. As they sit across from each other, encourage them to take turns explaining why they are upset. Then ask them to share ideas for easing the conflict. When they've cooled off, select solutions to try for peacefully solving the problem.

- **Create *grrrr* puppets.** When your child is growling with frustration and angrily gnashing his teeth, make puppets with the extra socks you have around. Add features with markers. Act out the problem and look for ways to solve it with the help of the puppets. You may wish to create a puppet theater by cutting a hole out of the bottom of a large open box, turning it on its side, and then placing it on a table. Let your child use his loud voice so he can work out some of his anger or frustration.

- **Find out the cause of the frustration.** Instead of pointing a finger at your child and asking her, "Why did you behave like that?" (pinching or grabbing a toy), try asking, "What made you so angry?" It may frustrate her less if she does not feel as though she is being blamed. Then, you can go ahead and help her work through her feelings.

RELATED BOOKS TO READ WITH CHILDREN

Bang, Molly. 1999. *When Sophie Gets Angry—Really, Really Angry.* New York: Scholastic.

Cook, Julia. 2011. *I Just Don't Like the Sound of NO! (How About MAYBE?): My Story about Accepting "No" for an Answer and Disagreeing…the Right Way!* Boys Town, NE: Boys Town Press.

Kaiser, Cecily. 2004. *If You're Angry and You Know It.* New York: Scholastic.

Spelman, Cornelia M. 2000. *When I Feel Angry.* Morton Grove, IL: Albert Whitman.

Steig, William. 2011. *Spinky Sulks.* New York: Square Fish.

7

COPING WITH **FEARS AND ANXIETIES**

Fear—a disturbing feeling caused by the notion of impending danger
Anxiety—worry and nervousness about what might possibly happen

Fears can sometimes be overwhelming and persistent for preschoolers. Some of the following types of fears and anxieties commonly appear in three- and four-year-olds, although individual children naturally develop at different rates:

- Three-year-olds are often frightened by costumed and masked characters because they have difficulty distinguishing between fantasy and reality.
- Three-year-olds may refuse to play the villain because they are anxious about actually turning into a burglar, for example, and being sent to prison.
- Three-year-olds often group together real fears and imaginary fears into a category of frightening objects.
- Four-year-olds learn through a transfer of information to be frightened of certain things, such as a mom's fear of spiders.

- Four-year-olds are curious about new experiences, and even though they might be a little anxious, they are willing to take risks and investigate.
- Four-year-olds can be fearful of anxiety-producing events that they have no control over, such as a natural disaster, war, and divorce.

Now let's look at some examples of how preschoolers' fears and anxieties might arise and play out in the classroom.

As a group of preschoolers water their garden with a hose, a black garter snake suddenly slithers out from under a big pumpkin leaf. Four-year-olds Rosa and Ami immediately run away, screaming hysterically. Three-year-old Nelson goes to tell the teacher about the snake. Charles, a four-year-old, watches the snake rapidly move away, and then he follows it with great curiosity. In a bold, defensive move, four-year-old Richard decides to yell at the snake. Then he grabs the hoe to see if he can hit the snake and scare it away permanently.

The preschoolers cope with the same situation in the garden in very different ways for individual reasons. Let's examine why the snake that frightens Rosa and Ami fascinates their classmate Charles. One child's temperament makes him react fearfully while another responds with bravery. Some personalities cause preschoolers to respond with too much fear, while others are not fearful enough.

In Rosa's case, her mom is terrified of snakes. She screams whenever she sees one and tells Rosa that they are nasty, dangerous creatures. Through this transfer of information, Rosa has vicariously learned to be frightened of snakes. Ami learns to withdraw from a scary situation because she is following her friend's lead. Both girls are exhibiting signs of being frightened as their hearts race, their tummies churn, and they have little nervous eye tics.

Nelson, a young preschooler, has learned from previous experiences that if you don't know what to do or need help, you ask your teacher or parent for assistance. Adults are usually able to fix things and offer comfort to relieve anxieties.

Fascinated by new experiences, Charles feels compelled to explore a curious situation. Even though the snake might be a little scary, Charles is willing to take a risk and investigate what's going on.

With their big, bold, loud personalities, four-year-olds, like Richard, enjoy showing off how brave they are. Knowing from a past experience that biting animals can hurt, he thinks he can protect his friends if he bullies the snake by yelling at it, hitting it, or chasing it away with the hoe.

Some fears may be specific to a particular child; however, at this preschool age many are typical for a certain stage. Three-year-olds, with their lack of experience, are still learning about the world. They are frequently frightened by the unfamiliar, such as when blood oozes from a cut or when a mustache and new glasses change someone's appearance. Things that are not whole, such as broken crayons or a doll with a missing arm, are disturbing for three-year-olds. Having difficulty distinguishing between reality and fantasy, they become anxious around costumed characters and people wearing masks. Halloween can be very scary for three-year-olds! With their vivid imaginations, four-year-olds become frightened by such things as thunder and lightning, strange animals, bugs, bathtub drains, moving shadows, and injections.

Fear of strange things is actually quite natural and can be a healthy behavior. Fear can help keep young children safe. For example, fear of power tools, biting animals, traffic, and fire can protect preschoolers from danger. Fear of being cut by sharp objects or climbing to great heights and then falling may help to stop three-year-olds and four-year-olds from taking unnecessary risks.

There are so many types of fears that cause preschoolers to feel anxious. There are unpredictable events, such as the sound of thunder and sudden flashing lights. Certain events that they have no control over are stressful and anxiety producing, such as natural disasters, war, divorce, and moving to a new home. And then there are the intangible fears of being abandoned or kidnapped. Because preschoolers take what we say literally, imagine what a young child is thinking when his mom or teacher says, "You must wear your sunscreen outdoors to play; otherwise, the hot sun will burn you up!"

It is so difficult for preschoolers to make a distinction between fantasy and reality. Three-year-olds and four-year-olds often bundle real fears (hissing snakes) and imaginary fears (dragons breathing fire) into a category of frightening objects. It is hard for them to tell whether dreams and fantasies are real or make-believe. For this reason, nightmares are extremely frightening, and some children do not want to close their eyes for sleep in case a monster comes and tries to steal them away in the dark.

At age three, my grandson Owen was terrified of the Easter Bunny after seeing this huge costumed creature at the mall. This frightening experience stayed with him, giving him nightmares and causing him to run away whenever he saw a bunny on the lawn or read a storybook in school about a rabbit. At his age, his behavior was not considered irrational, because he could not separate appearances from reality.

In a similar fashion, fueled by TV shows and movie fantasies, preschoolers may refuse to be evil characters during play because they do not wish to turn into criminals and be put in jail. They may love playing superheroes but be afraid of other outside forces.

Preschoolers often use their intuitive thinking to explain how the shadows that appear on the wall during nap time are scary supernatural creatures. Using animistic thinking, they give a personality to inanimate objects such as the shadows to suggest how these frightening things are trying to chase them.

Separation anxiety and school fears go hand in hand. As the preschooler gets ready for a first school experience, she may be afraid she'll get lost or her mom won't be able to find her. She may be anxious that she'll displease her teacher or parents because she can't do certain things, such as write her name or sit still. Or she may be anxious that no one will like her. The pressure to take a big-girl step and leave her familiar home environment can be very frightening.

Fortunately, most children seem to grow out of a majority of their fears. Verbal reassurances that you are there for them, as well as the physical support of sitting next to them and giving them protective pats or hugs, can go a long way to help reduce their anxieties. Removing the fear-causing event or objects also can help preschoolers cope.

WHAT YOU CAN DO

- **Plan ahead with the child.** Ask the child what he wants to do to try to make him feel less frightened. He might say, "Run away from a bully," or "Blow a whistle to scare away a barking dog." Try reading a story about a visit to the dentist so he knows what to expect. Discuss his questions.

- **Don't ignore a child's fears.** And make sure others don't tease her. Reassure her with a calm voice and words. Give physical support by going with her to check out a scary event or object. She may need to sit next to you during story time if you are reading a book about one of her fears (such as dogs or balloons). If she looks particularly anxious, she may need extra hugs to build her confidence. Respectfully allow her to master the fear at her own pace.

- **Work through something scary.** If a child is afraid of a large costumed character, such as the Easter Bunny at the mall, ask a parent to bring in a pet so the child can see at a distance that a real bunny is small and gentle. Try making a paper plate mask so the child can hold it up in front of his face, but not cover it, to act out fun, make-believe scenes.

- **Explore themes that reflect preschoolers' fears.** It is helpful for children to be introduced to the facts and encouraged to examine things they are afraid of. At Halloween, bones and skeletons were always a scary topic, so my classes would visit my husband's archaeology lab. Later, they'd set up their own boneyard in the sandbox and compare X-rays in the science center. One group painted wiggly bony bodies at the easel.

- **Use pretend play to reduce anxieties.** Provide real props—such as firefighting equipment, medical tools, and pet leashes and water bowls—so children can have an opportunity to practice with friends how they might act in a scary situation. Ask parents and community volunteers to contribute uniforms and artifacts for the dramatic play center. To help preschoolers understand what is real and what is not, encourage them to bring in costumes from home. Then talk about how the costumes transform children when they step inside.

OTHER ASPECTS TO CONSIDER—ALERTS

- **Weigh the intensity of the child's fears.** If the child's fears seem extreme or irrational and persist for an abnormal length of time, she may be developing a phobia (5 percent to 10 percent of children may have phobias). If her fears interfere with functioning normally at school or home, such as with making friends or sleeping, consider working with a counselor or psychologist for helpful suggestions.

- **Soothe nighttime fears.** In the first hour of sleep, night terrors may wake up the child in a panicky state. He'll usually not remember this. Comfort him and stay with him until he falls back asleep. In the early morning hours, a preschooler may have a scary nightmare. Often he has difficulty going back to sleep and may have clear memories of the frightening content. The nightmares usually have something to do with a problem or event troubling the child. Be a good listener and talk about his dream if he wants to.

- **Do not use fear as a form of discipline.** Sometimes adults try to scare children to control their behavior. They may say, "Santa is always watching you. If you do something bad, he won't bring you presents." Or they may threaten, "You'll sit by yourself alone in the corner away from all the other children if you don't use the playdough nicely." Using fear in this way can make preschoolers afraid of other things if they are pressured to feel they are displeasing adults.

ACTIVITIES FOR PARENTS TO TRY AT HOME

- **Minimize exposure to frightening things.** Preview TV programs to make sure they are appropriate. Watch together if shows seem a little scary. Always encourage your child to turn off a program when she is afraid. Discuss with your child why a certain aspect of a program frightened her. Talk about whether the scary thing was real or make-believe. Give her crayons and paper instead of a coloring book if she's anxious about staying in the lines.

- **Develop bedtime coping strategies.** So the room is not dark, use a night-light. Keep a flashlight handy for last-minute monster checks under the bed. "Go away monster spray" (scented water in a spray bottle) works well, too. A monster guard (a big stuffed animal) posted at the door can be a very friendly ally. And there's nothing like hugs and back rubs as you snuggle in for the night.

- **Offer a secure setting.** To relieve anxieties and help your child feel safe, make sure her environment is familiar and comfortable. Routines help with consistency. Indicate safety zones where she can go if play becomes too loud or frightening. Give her a special word to use (such as *pizza*) if she no longer wants to be a participant.
- **Try out coping mechanisms.** Take deep breaths, and then slowly let them out to relax. Call scary things by silly names (a spider becomes a "loopie-doopie") to reduce their perceived power. Put the child in control by letting him loudly shake pennies in a covered metal can to scare the intimidating thing away. If your child is afraid, encourage him to hum or sing a little song. In this way, he can concentrate on his singing instead of his fear, and maybe he'll banish the scary thing.
- **Designate a lost and found.** Becoming lost is frightening for a child and his parents. In strange places, work out a prior plan, such as a distinct place to meet (the clock tower) if lost. Put your cell-phone number in your child's pocket. At Disney World, our lost grandson Owen handed the card to a mom with three kids. We had an instant reunion and smiles all around!

RELATED BOOKS TO READ WITH CHILDREN

Atinuke. 2015. *Double Trouble for Anna Hibiscus.* San Diego: Kane Miller.

Brown, Margaret Wise. 1972. *The Runaway Bunny.* New York: HarperCollins.

Emberley, Ed. 1992. *Go Away, Big Green Monster!* Boston: Little, Brown.

Hendry, Diana. 1999. *The Very Noisy Night.* New York: Dutton's Children's Books.

Mayer, Mercer. 1968. *There's a Nightmare in My Closet.* New York: Puffin Books.

Zolotow, Charlotte. 1989. *The Storm Book.* New York: HarperTrophy.

8

DEVELOPING A SENSE OF HUMOR

Sense of humor—being able to appreciate the amusing or comical

Preschoolers enjoy using silly words, drawing silly pictures, and making silly movements. If they get a laugh in response, you will likely see more of the same behavior. You can expect to see some of the following types of attempts at humor among preschoolers.

- Three-year-olds find crazy, mixed-up, incongruous things very funny, such as a dog's head on a pig's body.
- Three-year-olds love to share silly stuff with their favorite adults.
- Three-year-olds enjoy wild, outrageous physical activities, such as dancing in the rain.
- Four-year-olds find playing with their food, such as turning an orange section into a goofy smile, quite humorous.
- Four-year-olds roar at slapstick comedy in cartoons and on TV.
- Four-year-olds need to be able to laugh off fears such as bleeding from a scratch.

Let's look at some of the types of silly incidents that you might encounter with the preschoolers in your care and what influences their behaviors.

Laughing, three-year-old Adam asks Ms. Gentry, his teacher, who is sitting on a couch with her right leg tucked under her skirt, "What happened? You only have one leg now!" They share in this surprise together. Then Adam laughs again when she uncurls her leg from its hiding place and it suddenly appears. Later, Adam teases her by stating, "You are a boy." Ms. Gentry replies, "No, I am a girl." Smiling, Adam keeps insisting, "You are a boy like me." Giggling, he finally explains, "That's because you have short hair just like me!"

As three-year-olds become more social, they delight in sharing silly stuff with special adults, such as their teacher. They also love to mimic an adult's laughter as they slowly learn to develop their sense of humor. They particularly enjoy laughing at things that they consider incredible or absurd, such as Ms. Gentry temporarily having one leg or being a boy.

Three-year-olds really love a good joke on themselves, especially if something ridiculous happens accidentally. For instance, Elijah piles wooden blocks into a cardboard box. Then he picks up the box. The bottom suddenly breaks open, and the blocks come tumbling out all over the floor again. Surprised at this event, Elijah howls with laughter.

The goofier the better! With their friends, three-and-a-half-year-olds love to have fun doing wild, outrageous physical activities, such as noisily stomping and jumping up and down barefoot in mud puddles. Feeling silly, three girls chase each other around by flapping their arms like ducks and mooing like cows. Preschoolers find mixed-up, incongruous things such as these crazy animals oh so funny.

Preschoolers love playing with words and sounds. Nevaeh experiments with rhyming words, real and made up. Giggling, she calls her doll "Fatty Patty" and delights in chanting a silly hand-washing song, "Soapy, dopey, popey." Preschoolers roar when someone mislabels words, such as calling a "head" a "bed." Four-year-olds enjoy playfully stringing together words in nonsensical ways. You might hear something like, "Sanjay drives a bumpkin pumpkin bus to munch-a-lunch town." Three-and-a-half-year-olds can't stop laughing when a buddy tells a story in a very high, squeaky voice, then downshifts to add funny, deep, booming sounds.

Preschoolers find playing with their food humorous, even though adults may not. Chuckling, Ariana picks up her banana and calls Jayla on her pretend "banana phone." Jayla is having her own fun distorting words and teasing Ariana by grabbing her "pamama phone."

Actions and words that three-year-olds and four-year-olds find funny are frequently annoying to adults. However, bathroom humor is high on many four-year-olds' lists of really silly stuff. They gleefully call each other "poopy head." And they giggle knowingly while using words for private body parts. When their teacher reads their favorite hysterically funny book, *Parts* (2000) by Tedd Arnold, to the class it appeals to their sense of humor as the boy fears his body parts are loosening up and falling apart.

Slapstick comedy in cartoons sets off waves of laughter in preschoolers. *Sesame Street* is popular with this young crowd because of the surprise actions and silly antics of the personable characters with their oddball voices. Shows like this help preschoolers laugh about some of their own fears. Four-year-olds need to be able to laugh off fears about things such as death or bleeding. For instance, during a warm summer day in Vermont, my grandson Owen said to me, "Ready? I have a joke. Go outside. There is a little snow dog out there." Outdoors, I looked all around. Finally, I asked, "Where?" Falling over with laughter, Owen said, "It died!" (It melted.)

Older four-year-olds think that telling a joke is pretty cool—even if they don't truly understand the logic behind it. They may have some difficulty actually delivering the punch line, but they love to laugh with others anyway and be a part of the fun.

What You Can Do

- **Be open and playful.** Preschoolers will appreciate it if you laugh at their jokes. Even if you've already heard them a dozen times, they are still funny to them. One of my four-year-old jokesters, Danny, loved to tell this silly joke over and over: "Did you hear about the two eggs? Too (two) bad!" Preschoolers love repetition and learn to develop their sense of humor from practice.

- **Help children be insiders.** It's a good feeling when they get a joke. It's important for them to understand the difference between real and fantasy in order to be able to identify silly behavior. For example, this helps them see the humor in a surprise action such as a monkey eating with chopsticks.

- **Create silly stories.** Develop humorous story lines such as having the prince wear his pants on his head. Use different funny voices. Speak slowly or in a singsong voice. Try high squeaky voices or ones that are very low. Use over-the-top, exaggerated motions or try silly, slow-motion actions. Add hilarious hats and dress-up clothes and other outrageous props. Act out the story, and then record a video for funny replays.

- **Draw ridiculous pictures together.** Change characteristics or behaviors to create amusing drawings. Remove a feature (a bike without wheels), reverse an item (moose antlers on a bunny and long ears on a moose), and change shapes or sizes (a triangular TV). Share these in a goofy picture gallery. Ask others to title the pictures for more laughs.
- **Write nonsense songs.** Use silly rhymes ("tutti-fruitti—what a cutie") or have preschoolers use made-up words. Pretend to be singing animals. There is nothing sillier than a chanting chicken or a chorus of chipmunks. The preschoolers might like to add several crazy dancing crabs to go along with their goofy lyrics. Record the silly songs for future funny sing-alongs.

Other Aspects to Consider—Alerts

- **Differences may not be funny.** Frequently, a young child will point or laugh at someone or something she thinks is funny because it looks strange. For example, a child may find it humorous to watch an unsighted person walking slowly and tapping a white cane because she doesn't understand the reason for this behavior. You will need to guide the child to help her learn about differences so she understands that it would be unkind to laugh about certain things that really are not funny.
- **Accidents can be serious.** When something happens accidently to another child, such as tripping on the rug and then falling down and getting hurt, you will need to model kindness and empathetic behavior toward the injured child if the class laughs.
- **Bathroom humor can be inappropriate.** It's quite normal for preschoolers to use potty words and think this is funny. Usually you can simply ignore their bathroom talk. However, if the words are insulting or really gross, such as calling a child's chocolate birthday cupcakes "piles of poop," you will need to discuss how this might be hurtful to others.

Activities for Parents to Try at Home

- **Follow your child's lead.** Watch his reaction so jokes and silly happenings are on his level. Use both verbal and physical types of humor. You could play tickle games and while giggling say, "I'm going to get your tummy!" Repeat his personal nonsense rhymes. He'll love you for it!
- **Initiate silly surprises.** Share unexpected things to spark your child's sense of humor. For example, put socks on her hands for gloves or hang flip-flops from your ears. Give her elephant hugs and goldfish kisses. Your child may try out some silly surprises on you, too, such as putting your hoop earrings on her stuffed bunny's ears. She may find it humorous to attach sticky notes to her wiggly puppy. Silly surprises can pop up everywhere!

Emotional Development of Three- and Four-Year-Olds

- **Find funny pictures.** Take pictures of humorous family activities (licking icing off fingers or hanging upside down). Put them in a family album to share the silliness. We have generations of silly photos on a wall at our summer cottage to enjoy forever. You could also create funny comic strips using family faces.

- **Play the wrong-name game.** Call Alex by the name Taylor. Ask for opposite items, such as jam instead of mustard for a hotdog. Sing, "Row, row, row your airplane." All of this silly fun will generate lots of laughs.
- **Make transitions fun.** Moving from place to place can be uninteresting for a crabby kid. Encourage him to try being a "delicate dancing dinosaur" or a "silly slithering snake" to get where he needs to go. If you say, "No giggling," see how long he can keep from laughing out loud.
- **Play "the funniest thing I ever . . . ."** When the family is together (riding in the car, sitting at the breakfast table, or waiting at a restaurant), play this game for a good laugh. Each person might tell about "the funniest thing I ever saw" (maybe a bird swimming in a puddle or a lady with pencils in her hair). Family members will surely giggle when they explain "the funniest thing I ever ate" (such as spaghetti without a fork, a melted ice cream cone, or fuzzy peaches). This humorous, entertaining family game can go on forever.

RELATED BOOKS TO READ WITH CHILDREN

Feiffer, Jules. 1999. *Bark, George*. New York: HarperCollins.

Parr, Todd. 2012. *The Underwear Book*. New York: Little, Brown Books for Young Readers.

Rosenthal, Amy Krouse, and Tom Lichtenheld. 2009. *Duck! Rabbit!* San Francisco: Chronicle Books.

Stone, Jon. 2004. *The Monster at the End of This Book*. New York: Golden Books.

Willems, Mo. 2003. *Don't Let the Pigeon Drive the Bus*. New York: Hyperion Books for Children.

LEARNING TO **RESOLVE** CONFLICTS

Resolving conflicts—working out peaceful solutions to problems or disputes

A s preschoolers interact with one another, they are bound to get into conflicts from time to time. The following snapshots can help you understand some common tendencies and challenges as three- and four-year-olds play and learn together, so you can better assist with conflict resolution.

- Three-year-olds, with their short attention spans, may decide to enter and leave many brief conflicts during the day.
- Three-year-olds frequently tell the teacher if they need help, or they may respond by hitting if they are very angry.
- Three-year-olds are inclined to argue over possessions.
- Four-year-olds know that school toys are supposed to be used by everyone and returned after a turn is taken.

- Four-year-olds may resort to name calling or bullying another child if they become frustrated when that child won't give up a possession.
- Four-year-olds are apt to become embroiled in power struggles related to control and gaining attention.

The following anecdotes will give you a better idea of the types of interactions that might be happening with preschoolers in your care and factors in their world that might be influencing their conflicts.

Ellie, a three-year-old, sits in the sandbox happily filling a pail with sand. Four-year-old Colin asks her, "Can I use the pail to carry sand?" Ellie replies, "No. It's mine!" Frowning, Colin tries to explain to her, "You need to share the pail. It belongs to everybody at school." Then Colin attempts to bargain. "I'll trade you two funnels for the pail." Glaring, Ellie refuses his offer by shaking her head and hugging the pail tightly. When the bargaining doesn't work, Colin informs Ellie, "Dummy! You know I'm stronger than you. I can take that pail away." Ellie ignores him.

The majority of preschool conflicts, such as this one, occur over possessions. Usually, the confrontation lasts only a minute. Three-year-olds, like Ellie, tend to be self-centered. So it is not uncommon for them to feel that if they are playing with an item at the time, then it is theirs. However, less egocentric four-year-olds, like Colin, know that school toys are supposed to be used by all of the children. The thought of giving a toy away is difficult and almost impossible for a three-year-old to understand because she has not had enough experience seeing that sharing a toy with someone is not necessarily a permanent giveaway. It will be returned to her when the person has taken his turn.

Being able to see things from another's viewpoint, four-year-olds, like Colin, and some older three-year-olds attempt to avoid conflict by using reciprocal behaviors. In addition to sharing and bargaining, they might try turn taking and compromising as positive ways to settle a problem regarding a possession.

If a young child does not have extensive language skills, she might react to a request much the same as Ellie by physically refusing with a head shake or by protectively guarding the object. Other nonverbal tactics are to ignore the appeal or scowl at the requester in the hope that he'll go away. Or she may decide to give up the item and simply walk away. When a preschooler becomes frustrated because the other child won't give up the desired possession, he might resort to name calling, verbally threatening, or bullying her. Even though all of these negative interactions seem to be unproductive, they do allow preschoolers an opportunity to experiment with a variety of emotions while learning how to navigate conflicts and relate to others.

Dressed in filmy scarves, Grace is pretending to be the bride, while Lucy is the bridesmaid. These four-year-olds are joyously dancing at the pretend wedding palace. After watching the celebration, three-and-a-half-year-old Claire asks if she can join them for some wedding cake. Grace responds, "No! You aren't dressed up for our beautiful wedding." Upset, Claire pulls off Grace's veil and runs to tattle to the teacher.

Another cause of conflict can be territorial issues over space. Frequently, a third child observes from the edge of a play activity and hopes to be included. Unfortunately, Claire's feelings were hurt when her request was rebuffed, and she felt insulted. Still slightly egocentric and not quite socially sophisticated enough to figure out how to allow a third party to join their special event, the four-year-olds responded by chasing Claire away. Their concern was not really about Claire's feelings.

With their short attention spans, three-year-olds have the potential to enter and leave many brief conflicts during the day as they seek exciting activities. Moving in and out of the conflict areas, they may respond by hitting if they are angry or telling the teacher if they need help. Sometimes, however, they are fortunate to be invited to join in and happily become part of the play, especially if they bring along an important prop.

Many three-year-olds are inclined to argue over possessions, and four-year-olds are apt to become embroiled in power struggles related to control and gaining attention. Bold, bossy, and loud, four-year-olds need to be the king or ride on the largest scooter. They like to be in charge and control their peers, especially if the peers are not quite as assertive. When they dictate various roles during play or command others to play a certain way, conflicts often arise. For instance, while working in the class garden, Conner decides to be in charge of watering while he assigns Wyatt to be Farmer Brown and hoe the weeds.

When Wyatt objects, Conner says gruffly, "Tough!" Then, he squirts him with the hose. Subdued, Wyatt succumbs to Conner's bullying and sullenly starts to hoe the weeds.

If the boys had tried out their negotiating skills, the results might have been quite different. After identifying the

Emotional Development of Three- and Four-Year-Olds

problem, then discussing and trying out various options (taking turns with the equipment, obtaining a second hose, or sharing the hose), their conflict might have been resolved with a much more positive, cooperative ending and everyone having fun!

What You Can Do

- **Don't jump right in.** Try not to intervene as children attempt to resolve their conflict, unless they might injure someone, break equipment, or go out of their way to intentionally hurt another child's feelings. Observe as they work the problem through, so they can develop self-confidence in their skills.
- **Teach negotiation skills.** With your help, older four-year-olds can learn how to negotiate to resolve problems: identify the problem, brainstorm solutions, select and try out an idea, and evaluate it. Then have a great time!
- **Help children access group play.** When a child desires to enter an activity, talk him through how to do it. For example, he might offer to bring his truck to the construction site. Or he might ask, "Do you need an ambulance driver?" If this doesn't seem to work, try some social engineering by giving the hesitant child and the group some prompts, such as "It looks like your restaurant could use a waiter. Dequan is available. He could use this pad and pencil."
- **Create rules together.** When conflicts occur over equipment or space, ask the children to help you determine rules, such as how many children should play. Ask how they will know when a turn is over. They might set a timer or limit the turn to three laps around the yard. So that all players are in agreement, create boundaries together. The boundary might be "as far as the big tree" or "stay on the blacktop." Making shared decisions can help minimize bickering.
- **Provide duplicates.** If conflicts arise over using certain popular items, such as balls, tricycles, dolls, or drums, provide additional ones to reduce waiting time. Demonstrate turn taking and sharing with the new toys.
- **Have a plan for dealing with biting.** Although toddlers are much more apt to try to resolve a conflict by biting, some young

three-year-olds may still explore this strategy. Besides frightening and hurting the intended victim, biting can really upset parents. If biting should occur, make sure both children are okay, and then send the child who bit to sit with another teacher. Next, calm the bitten child and take care of any wound (wash with soap and water, use a bandage, then apply a cool compress). Now, talk to the offending child and explain how biting hurts. Discuss other, more positive ways to settle a conflict: she can tell the other child what behavior she doesn't like, she can yell "stop" or "no" instead of reacting physically, or she can get the teacher. You will need to call the parents of both children. For confidentiality reasons, do not share the name of the child who bit with the victim's parents.

OTHER ASPECTS TO CONSIDER—ALERTS

- **Assess the conflict magnitude.** When young children are in competition for toys, space, or attention, they sometimes become physical and hit, push, kick, or even bite each other. If their conflict escalates, it is important for you to step in before someone gets hurt. Physical tactics are not uncommon for this age. However, if this seems to be the manner in which a child consistently tries to resolve a conflict, you need to work with him to model more peaceful ways of conflict resolution.
- **Watch for bullying.** If a preschooler seems to continually bully others—physically or verbally—to get her own way, you will need to have an immediate conference with her parents. She may need to meet with a counselor if this behavior continues.
- **Recognize challenges with sharing personal items.** Because they are still egocentric, three-year-olds have difficulty sharing their personal possessions, especially favorite items from home (such as a blanket or stuffed animal). This makes them feel vulnerable. They shouldn't be expected to share their special personal things unless they really want to. You might need to find a special place to store their prized possessions.

ACTIVITIES FOR PARENTS TO TRY AT HOME

- **Offer cooperative activities.** Show your preschoolers how much fun it is to work together. Provide materials such as puzzles and parquetry blocks. Have them participate in making a snack cooperatively by shaking cream in a jar to create butter or whipping up instant pudding.
- **Put special toys away.** Before a play date, remove toys your child simply can't share—such as a doll from Grandma or a favorite superhero. This will help eliminate squabbling and hurt feelings when the children play.

- **Support expression of feelings.** Encourage your child to practice verbalizing his thoughts by using hand puppets to act out sharing situations. Or draw faces on your hands with markers to represent different characters.
- **Talk through requests.** Emphasize with your preschooler that she should ask permission before she uses someone's belongings. Demonstrate talking in a pleasant voice instead of yelling to obtain something.
- **Replay real situations.** Use actual toys as props. Have your children take opposite roles (requesting an item and possessing an item) to see how the conflict feels from the other person's viewpoint. Then, switch roles.
- **Read fairy tales with conflicts.** During story time, read and act out "The Three Billy Goats Gruff." Discuss how they resolved their conflict with the troll. Is this a good way? How might they fix the problem in a more positive way?

RELATED BOOKS TO READ WITH CHILDREN

Dr. Seuss. 1984. *The Butter Battle Book.* New York: Random House Books for Young Readers.

Henkes, Kevin. 2001. *Sheila Rae's Peppermint Stick.* New York: Greenwillow.

Hoban, Russell. 1970. *A Bargain for Frances.* New York: Harper & Row.

Lionni, Leo. 1985. *It's Mine.* New York: Alfred A. Knopf.

Udry, Janice May. 1961. *Let's Be Enemies.* New York: Harper & Row.

10

COPING WITH SEPARATION AND LOSS

Separation—a circumstance when one person leaves another or when two things are moved apart

Loss—a feeling of sadness if someone or something is gone or taken away

ealing with separation and loss can be hard at any age, but preschoolers often don't understand the changes they are encountering. Consider some of the typical responses you will see among three- and four-year-olds as they deal with the emotions that surface during these types of situations:

- Three-year-olds may revert to familiar comfortable behaviors, such as holding a favorite teddy bear, to ease a painful separation.
- Three-year-olds enter into goodbye rituals, such as hugging Dad three times, to help soften the pangs of separation anxiety.
- Three-year-olds who are left behind are often as emotionally torn by the loss as the friend who is moving away.

- Four-year-olds can be confused by time-concept expectations about when a parent might return.
- Four-year-olds may find it difficult to comprehend that death is not reversible.
- Four-year-olds sometimes become very angry or upset with the parent who goes away.

The reaction to a transition, a separation, or a loss will depend on each child's temperament, influences, and experiences, among other factors. As you think about how to help and encourage the preschoolers in your care, look closer at some of these types of situations at home and school that three- and four-year-olds might need to navigate.

On the first day of preschool, wearing his new sneakers and colorful superhero backpack, Devin, an independent four-year-old, high-fives a greeting to Aiden, his buddy from last year's class. Then he turns and says, "See you later, alligator," as he waves goodbye to his mom at the door. Not having as easy a time separating from her dad, three-year-old

Jasmine clings tightly to her father's slacks for security. For additional comfort, she clutches her favorite "blankie" with the other hand. After the teacher encourages them to spend some time together reading a book, Jasmine blows her dad three kisses goodbye from the window. Then, Jasmine's teacher gently guides her to the sand table to play with a new friend, Zoe.

How well young children separate from their parents and form new attachments, such as in a new school setting, depends on each child's temperament, needs, and previous experiences, as can be seen from Devin's and Jasmine's school entries. Even when a child seems well adjusted, she may still revert to a familiar, comfortable behavior, such as thumb sucking. Having a special friend to relate to or a favorite place to settle into can help ease what might be a painful separation. Goodbye rituals (blowing kisses) and sharing intimate moments (reading a story) with a parent can soften separation anxiety. The bond of attachment to parents, teachers, and peers, which begins in the early childhood years, enables children to develop and maintain healthy emotional relationships.

Often school separations and transitions can also be difficult. For instance, when Juan moves from the toddler group to the three-year-old room, he is anxious and full of questions. "Will there be playdough?" "Can my teacher come with me?" Favorite toys, activities, and people are important to three-year-olds.

During the year, some children may move away after they have established wonderful friendships. It can be as difficult emotionally for the child who is moving as it is for a best friend who is staying behind and will miss him. Ms. Epting helped her class with such an impending separation by taking photos to share of the children doing favorite activities together for a class book and also a memory book for Jacob, who was moving. Later, she acknowledged the children's sadness about the loss of their friend and helped them send picture-letters to his new home.

For some preschoolers, separations from their parents may last a length of time. For example, Julie's mom travels frequently during the week on business. Because her dad spends lots of time caring for her, she tells him she loves him the most. Sometimes, Julie becomes angry with her mom when she goes away. Confused,

she thinks maybe this is her fault because she did something wrong. In school, Julie may appear out of sorts and need special attention from her teacher.

In today's world, where so many young children's lives are uprooted when their parents are deployed for military duty, they may experience various separation adjustments and stressors—moving, a parent's absence, living with grandparents. Three-year-olds and four-year-olds may worry that the other parent might leave them, too. If they see TV shows or hear the news about military engagements, they often worry about the deployed parent's safety as well as their own. You may see them acting out with violence during dramatic play or bombing their block creations. If daily routines and schedules get changed around, you'll need to be on the lookout for temper tantrums or regressive behavior, such as baby talk or soiled pants. You will need to help a child with time concepts. Instead of confusing four-year-old Carlos by telling him Daddy will return in a year, his teacher explained he'd be back around Halloween. Carlos remembered that Halloween was when he dressed up like a robot.

For a preschooler who is experiencing the effects of divorce, many of the same long-term issues of separation that occur with a parent's deployment apply. Except then the child has the expectation that the parent will return. This will not be true for a divorce.

Emotionally, preschoolers are vulnerable, and it is difficult for them to verbally express how they feel about their sense of loss and rejection when their parents decide to divorce.

Mrs. Barlow makes sure there are numerous quality books available about divorce for her preschoolers to read with her when they need to talk about their feelings on the topic. Mrs. Barlow is quick to observe when a child needs a security hug if she is sad because she misses the parent who no longer lives with her.

Because three-year-olds and four-year-olds are inclined to be self-centered, they may feel they have been responsible for their parents separating. Preschoolers do not want their parents to separate! It is difficult for them to see things from another's point of view, which makes it difficult for them to understand the concept of divorce.

When moving or divorce takes a preschooler away from someone he is close to or loves, he may feel just as distressed as if it were the painful permanence of death. Preschoolers are not always strangers to death. A young child may have experienced the death of a pet that was a beloved companion. Children see dead people on TV shows and read about them in fairy tales. However, they find it difficult to comprehend that death is not reversible. For instance, using her magical thinking, Eva tells her teacher as she deals out the Old Maid cards that she is waiting for her grandma to come back and play their favorite game. Knowing how literally preschoolers tend to take things, her teacher is careful not to tell Eva that her grandmother has "gone to sleep," which might make Eva frightened to go to sleep. She gently explains that when Eva's grandmother died, her body simply stopped working. She let Eva know that her grandmother can't come back, even though Eva loves her and wants her to return.

What You Can Do

- **Provide reassurances.** Often, a child who is angry and frustrated acts out physically because he can't verbalize his feelings. He may just be worried about who will take care of him. Instead of disciplining him, try to use calm words and gentle gestures to discuss his feelings and let him know you are there to support him.

- **Offer comfort.** Familiarity helps make transitions go more smoothly. Invite an anxious child to bring a familiar item (such as a blanket or teddy bear) to school for comfort. Provide a warm, cozy environment (such as a beanbag chair or quilt) in which to read a book together. Set up soothing centers with sand and water or cuddly stuffed animals.

- **Make time to talk.** Give a child one-on-one time to help her talk about her feelings and understand that the missing person is still a part of her life. If the person is working away from home or deployed, talk about that person's job. Try singing her special song. Together, make and share her favorite snack while chatting.

- **Validate children's feelings.** Offer interesting items for a child to use to write or draw messages to the absent person. Provide books to read so he can see how others approach similar problems. Display props and puppets in the dramatic play center so the child can act out family separation situations.

- **Find ways to communicate.** If a child is separated from someone for a period of time, you can help them stay in touch by sending photo postcards or emails. Mrs. Dickey's class learned about Iraq as they spoke with a child's father at a military post through Skype. Try creating a recording of the child telling a story or describing aspects of the day with the absent person. In the instance that a parent may be incarcerated, strict restrictions will apply about communicating. However, this child may find it comforting to draw pictures that can be sent or delivered during a visitation to her incarcerated parent.

Other Aspects to Consider—Alerts

- **Note excessive behavior.** It might be difficult for some preschoolers to handle their emotions concerning separation or loss. However, if extensive aggression occurs (such as hurting others or breaking materials), the child demonstrates an inability to separate (for example, hanging onto a parent's arm), or she is not making clear developmental progress after several months, you may need to suggest that the parents seek professional assistance for the child.

- **Be sensitive to grief.** Make sure you do not dismiss a child's sadness or fears of separation by telling him everything will be okay. If he does not work through it, the effects may be prolonged, and he may not be able to process the event and cope with the loss of a specific loved one.

- **Be aware of poor attachment capacity.** A child exhibiting this behavior may have difficulty emotionally and socially entering into a relationship with a teacher or caregiver. For example, she might have difficulty expressing emotions appropriately. You can do some research on attachment theory to find ways to assist children dealing with this challenge. They may also need professional help.

Activities for Parents to Try at Home

- **Be clear.** Help your child understand time concepts. Use visual reminders to show how long before the father's visitation time (use checks on a calendar) or when the mother's deployment ends (take a jelly bean from a jar each day).

- **Use concrete words.** Explain that "Mema died," instead of saying, "We lost Mema." Otherwise, the child might feel confused and want to go look for his grandmother. When you tell your young child that Aunt Betsy has gone to Heaven, this may not be easily understandable to your child because it is an abstract place. He cannot visit or see Heaven the way he can when he goes to the town of Bristol for ice cream.

- **Respond to questions.** It is normal for your child to ask multiple times for clarification: "Will Mommy come back?" "Who will care for me?" If your child asks why the separation or loss occurred, be honest. Explain: "Papa was very sick and his body stopped working." Or you might say: "Mommy has to go away for her job. It is not your fault."

- **Create reassuring rituals.** These help your child know what to expect. At school, blow two goodbye kisses at the door. Tell her you will pick her up after snack. Set up a special parent-child date night to talk to the separated parent by phone or Internet video chat. Ask the child to draw a picture-letter shout-out every Monday morning, and mail it together.

- **Make special memories.** Sing personal songs together on the way to school. Have a great goodbye picnic before deployment. On weekends, take little local field trips—walk along a stream, visit a horse farm. Create a scrapbook of things the family enjoyed with a relative who died.

- **Enlist others.** To make it easier to separate from you, arrange for a carpool buddy to enter the classroom with your child. Ask the teacher to help your child engage in an activity to help with the transition. Spend time with Nana, who can share interesting stories about Papa. Join a play group with other military children who have similar questions.

Related Books to Read with Children

Brown, Laurie Krasny. 1998. *When Dinosaurs Die: A Guide to Understanding Death.* Boston: Little, Brown Books for Young Readers.

Brown, Margaret Wise. 2016. *The Dead Bird.* New York: HarperCollins.

Lansky, Vicki. 1997. *It's Not Your Fault, KoKo Bear: A Read-Together Book for Parents and Young Children during Divorce.* Minnetonka, MN: Book Peddlers.

Magorian, Michelle. 1990. *Who's Going to Take Care of Me?* New York: Harper & Row.

Masurel, Claire. 2003. *Two Homes.* Cambridge, MA: Candlewick.

Rogers, Fred. 1988. *When a Pet Dies.* New York: Putnam.

11

MILESTONES IN
EMOTIONAL
DEVELOPMENT

As you reflect on the ideas and examples discussed in this book, it might help to have a summary of some important milestones in emotional development that you might see during a child's preschool years.

We have discussed these common behaviors in different chapters and looked at strategies for dealing with challenges and encouraging development in emotional skills. By recognizing young children's tendencies at these stages, you can become better equipped to help them manage their emotions and have successful interactions and positive experiences. Remember, however, that children develop at different rates, some more slowly or some more rapidly than others. These milestones for three- and four-year-olds are intended for use as helpful guidelines. Enjoy the progress you will see in preschoolers' emotional skills during their different stages of growth.

Skills	Three-Year-Olds	Four-Year-Olds
Kindness and empathy	• Egocentric, they may not be able to exhibit sympathy and may appear unkind. • They don't understand apologizing to show they're sorry for their actions.	• They are less egocentric and more aware of others' feelings; they're able to exhibit sympathy. • Instead of always focusing on possessions, they are beginning to enjoy helping friends.
Independence	• They like to sit next to the teacher or a parent for physical support and verbal suggestions. • With increased communication skills, they try to gain control with verbal assertions.	• Wanting to be self-reliant, they may not wish to accept adult help; they want to do things their way. • Confident and persistent, they love to jump in and experiment.
Shyness	• They react to visual fears; they may try to hide from characters in holiday costumes. • Introverted or shy children may feel more comfortable playing by themselves.	• If they feel threatened, they may not speak to others and are disinclined to ask for help. • They are afraid of not doing things perfectly; they fear criticism and rejection from classmates.
Confidence	• They are easily self-satisfied and delighted with small accomplishments. • They may find it comforting to converse with an imaginary friend who is a good listener while they do things together.	• Participating in rituals to anticipate what happens next can help build up their confidence. • They use fantasy play to feel in control and be powerful as they act out different scenarios.
Limits and risks	• They watch from a safe vantage point to see what others decide before attempting to take a risk. • When efforts do not turn out as expected, they may feel guilty about taking a risk.	• They love to be the center of attention and push everyone's buttons as they test limits and live on the edge. • They seem to balance their sense of adventure and desire for safety as they attempt something risky.
Anger and frustration	• They may feel lost and become upset and frustrated by large spaces. • They may become jealous and frown, whine, or physically act out when the teacher gives her attention to another student.	• They use avoidance of tasks or people as a means to escape from their frustrations. • They may use name calling and trading insults in order to try to reclaim their possessions.

Skills	Three-Year-Olds	Four-Year-Olds
Fears and anxieties	• They are frightened by the unfamiliar (oozing blood) and things that are not whole (a broken arm). • They learn from previous experience to ask adults for help because adults are usually able to fix things and offer comfort to relieve fear.	• Quite bold, they think they can protect their friends if they bully, yell at, or chase away frightening things. • Most are generally frightened by thunder and lightning, strange animals, bugs, moving shadows, and injections.
Humor	• They enjoy laughing at things they consider implausible or incredibly absurd. • They love to laugh at themselves when they do something accidentally that is ridiculous.	• They are fascinated with intentionally mislabeling objects or mispronouncing words in silly ways. • They enjoy using bathroom humor and giggling while using body-part words in shocking ways.
Conflicts	• They feel that if they are playing with a toy, it is theirs. It is difficult for them to understand that sharing is a temporary situation. • With limited language skills, they may react to a conflict nonverbally (ignoring the other child, physically guarding an item, or giving up the item).	• They attempt to avoid conflict by using reciprocal behaviors (sharing or turn taking). • They like to be in charge and control their peers, especially if their peers are not assertive.
Separation and loss	• It is important to have favorite toys or a special friend available to help ease transitions during separations. • Bewildered, egocentric children feel that maybe it is their fault that their parents have separated or left home.	• Using magical thinking, they wish that a loved one, such as a divorced parent, will come back home to live with them. • Taking things literally, they can be confused if concrete language is not used. For example, they will respond better to the phrasing "Papa died" than to "We have lost Papa."

INDEX

professional help for, 36

typical behaviors, 32–35

H

humor, sense of.

See sense of humor

I

imaginary friends, 24, 25

incarceration, 60

independence

activities for, 14–16

children's books related to, 16

and confidence, 13

defined, 12

milestones in, 64

typical behaviors, 12–14

instrumental dependency, 13

J

jokes, 47

See also sense of humor

K

kindness

activities for, 8–9, 10–11

children's books related to, 11

defined, 5

milestones in, 64

modeling for children, 10–11, 48

professional help for, 10

typical behaviors, 5–8

L

labels, avoiding, 20, 30

language

avoiding labels, 20, 30

and conflict resolution, 35, 55

and dealing with loss, 60

and expressing anger, 33

positive vs. negative, 9

and testing limits, 29

limits, testing

activities for, 29–31

children's books related to, 31

defined, 27

milestones in, 64

typical behaviors, 27–29

loss

activities for, 59–61

children's books related to, 62

defined, 56

milestones in, 65

professional help for, 60

typical behaviors, 56–59

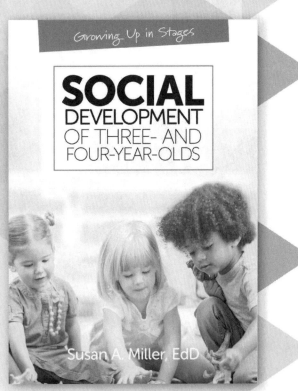